SAFETY AND RISK IN SOCIETY

PSYCHOLOGICAL TRAUMA AND FEELING OF DIRTINESS

SAFETY AND RISK IN SOCIETY

Additional books in this series can be found on Nova's website under the Series tab.

Additional e-books in this series can be found on Nova's website under the e-book tab.

SAFETY AND RISK IN SOCIETY

PSYCHOLOGICAL TRAUMA AND FEELING OF DIRTINESS

RYOTARO ISHIKAWA

New York

Copyright © 2015 by Nova Science Publishers, Inc.

All rights reserved. No part of this book may be reproduced, stored in a retrieval system or transmitted in any form or by any means: electronic, electrostatic, magnetic, tape, mechanical photocopying, recording or otherwise without the written permission of the Publisher.

For permission to use material from this book please contact us:
nova.main@novapublishers.com

NOTICE TO THE READER

The Publisher has taken reasonable care in the preparation of this book, but makes no expressed or implied warranty of any kind and assumes no responsibility for any errors or omissions. No liability is assumed for incidental or consequential damages in connection with or arising out of information contained in this book. The Publisher shall not be liable for any special, consequential, or exemplary damages resulting, in whole or in part, from the readers' use of, or reliance upon, this material. Any parts of this book based on government reports are so indicated and copyright is claimed for those parts to the extent applicable to compilations of such works.

Independent verification should be sought for any data, advice or recommendations contained in this book. In addition, no responsibility is assumed by the publisher for any injury and/or damage to persons or property arising from any methods, products, instructions, ideas or otherwise contained in this publication.

This publication is designed to provide accurate and authoritative information with regard to the subject matter covered herein. It is sold with the clear understanding that the Publisher is not engaged in rendering legal or any other professional services. If legal or any other expert assistance is required, the services of a competent person should be sought. FROM A DECLARATION OF PARTICIPANTS JOINTLY ADOPTED BY A COMMITTEE OF THE AMERICAN BAR ASSOCIATION AND A COMMITTEE OF PUBLISHERS.

Additional color graphics may be available in the e-book version of this book.

LIBRARY OF CONGRESS CATALOGING-IN-PUBLICATION DATA

ISBN: 978-1-63463-319-2

Published by Nova Science Publishers, Inc. † *New York*

CONTENTS

Preface		**vii**
Chapter 1	Sexual Assault and Mental Disorders	**1**
Chapter 2	Fear of Contamination in Obsessive-Compulsive Disorder	**11**
Chapter 3	Mental Contamination	**21**
Chapter 4	Sexual Assault and Mental Contamination	**27**
Chapter 5	Assessment of Mental Contamination	**37**
Chapter 6	Cognitive Vulnerability of Mental Contamination	**47**
Chapter 7	Role of Washing Behavior in Mental Contamination	**55**
Chapter 8	Mental Contamination and Low Self-esteem	**63**
Chapter 9	Clinical Implications	**71**
Acknowledgments		**81**
References		**83**
Index		**95**

PREFACE

In this book, I will explain some topics about (a) unwanted sexual experiences, such as sexual assault; (b) the feeling of dirtiness and impurity; (c) post-traumatic stress disorder; and (d) obsessive-compulsive disorder. This book focuses particularly on mental contamination, which refers to the feeling of dirtiness following experiences of ill treatment or sexual assault. Mental contamination has also been found to be prominent in victims of sexual assault and in patients with post–traumatic stress disorder (PTSD). As behavioral consequences of the feeling of mental contamination, victims of sexual assault suffering feelings of mental contamination might show excessive washing behavior, and may develop Obsessive-Compulsive Disorder (OCD).

In addition, I will discuss an effective cognitive behavioural therapy to improve post-traumatic reactions to sexual assault and obsessive-compulsive disorder with mental contamination.

Ryotaro Ishikawa, Ph.D.
University of Tokyo, Japan,
Department of Cognitive and Behavioral Science,
Graduate School of Arts and Sciences.
Email: ishikamyr124@gmail.com

Chapter 1

SEXUAL ASSAULT AND MENTAL DISORDERS

ABSTRACT

Victims/survivors of sexual assault may experience severe feelings of anxiety, stress, fear, or depression. This chapter demonstrates some mental health problems that sexual assault victims may experience.

(a) *Depression*: depression is a natural response to stressful situations. However, depression becomes something more than just a natural response to a stressful situation when the symptoms last for more than two weeks.
(b) *Rape trauma syndrome*: there are three phases to rape trauma reactions, such as acute phase, outward adjustment phase, and resolution phase.
(c) *Post-traumatic stress disorder* (PTSD): studies of assault victims have emphasized the roles of negative appraisals of trauma memories in maintaining the symptomatology of PTSD, and disorganized trauma memories in the development of PTSD.

INTRODUCTION

The sequelae of sexual assault affects the psychological, emotional, social, interpersonal, and financial domains in the short and long terms. This chapter describes some sexual victimization surveys, and some psychological distress and mental disorders that sexual assault victims may experience.

SEXUAL VICTIMIZATION SURVEYS

Sexual assault constitutes both physical and mental violence, and it is not easily recovered from. The National Crime Victimization Survey conducted by the U.S. Department of Justice revealed that in 2010, U.S. residents aged 12 or older experienced an estimated 18.7 million violent and property crime victimizations [1]. According to the survey, these criminal victimizations in 2010 included an estimated 3.8 million violent victimizations, 1.4 million serious violent victimizations, 14.8 million property victimizations, and 138,000 personal thefts. Almost 188,380 of the 1.4 million serious violent crimes were sexual assaults, including rape.

In Japan, Konishi [2] investigated sexual victimization in a sample of 430 Japanese university students. She asked about the lifetime prevalence of sexual victimization using a questionnaire. Results showed that half of the female sample had experienced victimization in the form of sexual molestation or exhibitionism. The proportion of students who had experienced rape was 1.8%. This study showed that there were many victims of childhood sexual victimization and that most of them regarded their experiences as very painful. Sasagawa et al. [3] further investigated the rate of sexual victimization in Japanese adult women. To assess the prevalence of sexual victimization, self-report questionnaires were sent to 666 Japanese adult women. Their results showed that 73.9% of the sample (n = 494) had experienced sexual victimization; 31.4% reported experiencing verbal harassment (being abused or harassed verbally), 58.4% reported experiencing sexual molestation (forced touching, fondling, or grabbing of any part of the body, such as sexual organs, buttocks, breasts, or mouth), 37.2% reported experiencing exhibitionism (being forced to look at a sexual object), and 6.9% reported experiencing rape (i.e., forced engagement in sexual intercourse, including vaginal, anal, or oral penetration by the offender). Sasagawa et al. also found that sexual molestation and exhibitionism tended to be perpetrated by a stranger, while verbal sexual harassment and rape was more often perpetrated by non-strangers, including the victim's family members, relatives, friends, and teachers [3]. Only 6.5% of the 418 victims who suffered the most upsetting victimization had reported it to the police, suggesting that such victimizations are rarely reported to police and remain unknown to society. They concluded that, to obtain comprehensive information, sexual victimization surveys should be administered repeatedly at college campuses.

DEPRESSION

Victims of rape and sexual assault can experience many emotional and psychological reactions. One of the most common symptoms is depression. These feelings are a natural response to stressful situations. However, depression becomes something more than just a natural response to a stressful situation when the symptoms last for more than two weeks. Therefore, anyone who experiences five or more symptoms of depression over the course of two weeks should consider talking to a therapist about what they are experiencing. The typical symptoms of depression include:

Chronic daily sadness
Unexplained crying spells
Significant changes in weight or appetite
A lack of energy
Chronic fatigue
Sleeping difficulties (insomnia, hypersomnia, fitful sleep, etc.)
Loss of pleasure in previously enjoyable activities, social withdrawal
Feelings of worthlessness, hopelessness, or guilt
Pessimism or indifference
Distractedness
Irritability, worry, anger, agitation, or anxiety
Suicidal ideation or attempt

These depressive symptoms can affect people of any age, gender, race, ethnicity, or religion.

RAPE TRAUMA SYNDROME [4]

This describes a normal human reaction to an extremely stressful event. There are three phases to rape trauma reactions.

Acute Phase. The acute phase of the reaction occurs immediately after the assault and usually lasts between a few days and several weeks. Many victims experience this acute phase, which is characterized by mental and physical dysfunction. Victims experience various symptoms of severe, acute psychological pain, as follows:

Crying all day
Dissociation
Fear of getting angry
Insomnia
Sensitivity
Strong feelings of hopelessness
Inability to concentrate on work and daily life
Distrust in others, feeling defensive
Insensitivity to feelings

Outward Adjustment Phase. Victims resume what appears to be their "normal" life, but inside they are still suffering considerable turmoil. The Rape & Abuse Incest National Network (RAINN) suggests that victims typically use five primary coping techniques during this phase:

Minimization: Victims pretend that everything is fine or convince themselves that "it could have been worse."

Dramatization: Victims cannot stop talking about the assault; it dominates victim's life and identity.

Suppression: Victims refuse to remember the event and act as if it did not happen.

Explanation: Victims analyze what happened, what they did, and what the rapist was thinking/feeling.

Flight: Victims try to avoid the pain using behavioral strategies such as moving, changing jobs, changing appearance, or changing relationships.

Resolution Phase. During this phase, the experience of sexual assault is no longer the central focus of the victim's life. While victims may recognize that they will never forget the experience, pain, and negative emotion, they often will begin to accept the trauma as part of their life and choose to move on.

Typically, most victims experience each of these phases. However, while there are phases, it is not a linear progression and the process is different for each victim; victims may take steps forward and backwards during their healing process.

Post-Traumatic Stress Disorder

The clinical diagnosis of post-traumatic stress disorder (PTSD) has helped to acknowledge the significance of the harm caused to people who have been sexually assaulted and the extent of the violation they have experienced. PTSD is a psychiatric label for a collection of psychological symptoms following a traumatic event (see the Diagnostic and Statistical Manual of Mental Disorders, 5th ed. [DSM-5] [137] for a full clinical definition and criteria [5]. PTSD is not a rare or unusual occurrence; in fact, many people experience PTSD as a result of a traumatic experience such as rape or sexual assault. A victim may be experiencing PTSD if she/he has experienced the following symptoms for at least a month:

a) **Stressor:** the person was exposed to: death, threatened death, actual or threatened serious injury, or actual or threatened sexual violence, as follows:

Direct exposure.

Witnessing, in person.

Indirectly, by learning that a close relative or close friend was exposed to trauma.

If the event involved actual or threatened death, it must have been violent or accidental.

Repeated or extreme indirect exposure to aversive details of the event(s), usually in the course of professional duties (e.g., first responders, collecting body parts; professionals repeatedly exposed to details of child abuse). This does not include indirect non-professional exposure through electronic media, television, movies, or pictures.

b) Intrusion symptoms: the traumatic event is persistently re-experienced in the following ways (one required).

Recurrent, involuntary, and intrusive memories. Note: Children older than six may express this symptom in repetitive play.

Traumatic nightmares. Note: Children may have frightening dreams without content related to the trauma(s).

Dissociative reactions (e.g., flashbacks) which may occur on a continuum from brief episodes to complete loss of consciousness. Note: Children may reenact the event in play.

Intense or prolonged distress after exposure to traumatic reminders.

Marked physiologic reactivity after exposure to trauma-related stimuli.

c) **Avoidance:** Persistent effortful avoidance of distressing trauma-related stimuli after the event (one required).

Trauma-related thoughts or feelings.

Trauma-related external reminders (e.g., people, places, conversations, activities, objects, or situations).

d) **Negative alterations in cognitions and mood: negative alterations in cognitions and mood that began or worsened after the traumatic event (two required).**

Inability to recall key features of the traumatic event (usually dissociative amnesia; not due to head injury, alcohol, or drugs).

Persistent (and often distorted) negative beliefs and expectations about oneself or the world (e.g., "I am bad," "The world is completely dangerous").

Persistent distorted blame of self or others for causing the traumatic event or for resulting consequences.

Persistent negative trauma-related emotions (e.g., fear, horror, anger, guilt, or shame).

Markedly diminished interest in (pre-traumatic) significant activities.

Feeling alienated from others (e.g., detachment or estrangement).

Constricted affect: persistent inability to experience positive emotions.

e) **Alterations in arousal and reactivity: trauma-related alterations in arousal and reactivity that began or worsened after the traumatic event (two required).**

Irritable or aggressive behavior

Self-destructive or reckless behavior

Hypervigilance

Exaggerated startle response

Problems in concentration

Sleep disturbance

f) **Duration:** Persistence of symptoms (in Criteria B, C, D, and E) for more than one month.

g) **Functional significance:** significant symptom-related distress or functional impairment (e.g., social, occupational).

h) **Exclusion:** disturbance is not due to medication, substance use, or other illness.

Specify if: With dissociative symptoms.

In addition to meeting criteria for diagnosis, an individual experiences high levels of either of the following in reaction to trauma-related stimuli:

Depersonalization: experience of being an outside observer of or detached from oneself (e.g., feeling as if "this is not happening to me" as if one were in a dream).

Derealization: experience of unreality, distance, or distortion (e.g., "things are not real").

Specify if: With delayed expression.

Full diagnosis is not met until at least six months after the trauma(s), although onset of symptoms may occur immediately.

WHAT ARE FLASHBACKS?

When victims experience flashbacks, memories of past traumas feel as if they are taking place in the current moment. These memories can take many forms: dreams, sounds, smells, images, bodily sensations, or overwhelming emotions. This re-experience of the assault often seems to arise out of nowhere, blurring the lines between past and present and leaving the individual feeling anxious, scared, or powerless. It can also trigger other emotions that were felt at the time of the trauma. Typically, flashbacks are mild and brief—a passing moment. However, others may be powerful and longer in duration. Some victims may not even realize that they are having a flashback; they may feel faint or dissociate, which means that their thoughts and feelings may become separate from their immediate reality.

COGNITIVE THEORY OF PTSD

Studies of cognitive theory of PTSD emphasized the roles of (A) negative appraisals of trauma memories in maintaining the symptomatology of PTSD, and (B) disorganized trauma memories in the development of PTSD [12-19].

(A) Negative Appraisals of Trauma

Several studies have suggested that cognitive appraisals play an important role in the persistence of PTSD. These have linked the severity of PTSD to specific negative beliefs about the self and the world, to the nature of the traumatic memory, or to both negative beliefs and the nature of the memory [6-11]. Ehlers and Clark [12] found that victims who go on to suffer persistent PTSD process the trauma in such a way that it leads to a sense of "serious current threat." They suggested that this sense of threat is affected by the individual's appraisals of the trauma and its sequelae. Appraisals about perceived threat generate strong emotions, such as anxiety, anger, shame, or guilt, as well as arousal symptoms [13]. Perceived threats can be focused externally (e.g., "Nowhere is safe," or "I cannot rely on other people.") or internally ("I can't trust my own judgments," "I am going mad," or "It was my fault."). Such appraisals also motivate the person to engage in maladaptive or avoidance behavior to control the threat. These behaviors are control strategies that may themselves exacerbate the PTSD symptoms. For example, rape victims who believe they will go mad unless they control their intrusive thoughts or flashbacks make intentional efforts to suppress trauma-related thoughts, which has the paradoxical effect of intensifying their intrusions [14-16]. Other control strategies may maintain PTSD symptoms by preventing the disconfirmation of negative beliefs and appraisals or by preventing change in the traumatic memory. For instance, victims who ensure they are never alone or who change their appearance to prevent unwelcome advances may exacerbate the belief that they would have been assaulted again if they had not taken these protective actions. Dunmore et al. [13] also found that cognitive appraisals significantly predict PTSD severity. These cognitive appraisals are as follows:

a) Cognitive processing style during the assault:
   i. Mental defeat (e.g., "I didn't feel like I was a human being anymore." "I mentally gave up.")
   ii. Mental confusion (e.g., "I couldn't believe this was happening to me." "My mind went blank.")
   iii. Detachment (e.g., "I automatically shut down and detached from what was happening.")

b) Appraisal of assault sequelae:
  i. Appraisal of trauma symptoms (e.g., "My reactions since the assault mean that I must be losing my mind.")
  ii. Perceived negative responses of others (e.g., "People who I thought would stand by me have let me down." "I feel like other people are ashamed of me now.")
  iii. Permanent change (e.g., "I will never recover." "My life has been destroyed by the assault." "I feel like I don't know myself anymore.")

c) Negative beliefs about self and the world (e.g., "I cannot trust my own judgments." "The world is dark and evil." "There is no justice in the world.")

(B) Disorganized Trauma Memories

The sense of current threat can also be determined by the nature of the traumatic memory itself. It has been suggested that persistent PTSD is associated with traumatic memories that are poorly elaborated and integrated into existing autobiographical memories [9][17-19]. Poor elaboration and incorporation of traumatic memories may account for the difficulty some PTSD sufferers have in intentionally recalling aspects of the memory, which in turn allows trauma-related cues to trigger a re-experiencing of the symptoms and intense emotions. When memories are poorly elaborated, the incorporation of information that might disconfirm negative appraisals is also hampered.

CONCLUSION

This chapter illustrated that victims of rape and sexual assault can experience many emotional and psychological distress, such as depression. PTSD is a psychiatric label for a collection of psychological symptoms following a traumatic event. Cognitive theory of PTSD suggested that cognitive appraisals play an important role in the persistence of PTSD. These have linked the severity of PTSD to specific negative beliefs about the self and the world, to the nature of the traumatic memory, or to both negative beliefs and the nature of the memory. In addition, persistent PTSD is associated with traumatic memories that are poorly elaborated and integrated into existing autobiographical memories.

Chapter 2

FEAR OF CONTAMINATION IN OBSESSIVE-COMPULSIVE DISORDER

ABSTRACT

Obsessive-compulsive disorder (OCD) is an anxiety disorder characterized by recurrent and disturbing thoughts called obsessions and/or repetitive, ritualized behaviors that the person feels the urge to perform called compulsions. The fear of contamination (e.g., "I avoid using public toilets because I am afraid of disease or contamination") features prominently in approximately half of all cases of OCD. This chapter demonstrated the differences between OCD and neat freaks, and explains a number of instruments to assess of OCD symptoms. Finally, cognitive theory of OCD indicated that some cognitive appraisals can result in the fear of contamination and an urge to wash.

INTRODUCTION

OCD is an anxiety disorder characterized by recurrent and disturbing thoughts called obsessions and/or repetitive, ritualized behaviors that the person feels the urge to perform called compulsions. Obsessions can take the form of intrusive thoughts, images, and impulses that the patient does not want. For example, obsessions include concerns about contamination (e.g., fear of contamination, germs, or serious illness), safety/harm (e.g., being responsible for a fire), unwanted aggressive action (e.g., unwanted images or thoughts of harming a loved one), unacceptable sexual or religious thoughts (e.g., thoughts about raping a child), and the need for symmetry or exactness.

Common compulsions include excessive cleaning, washing, checking, ordering, arranging rituals, counting, repeating routine activities, and hoarding (e.g., collecting useless items). Most compulsions are observable behaviors (e.g., hand washing), although some are unobservable mental rituals, such as mental checking or covert checking rituals. Mental checks are often accompanied by thoughts such as "did I do it the right way," "am I feeling the right way," or "did I do this for the right reason?". OCD affects roughly 1%–2.5% of the general population [5]. The World Health Organization [20] ranked OCD as the tenth leading cause of disability worldwide. In Japan, the national prevalence of OCD is about 2%, as it is in the U.S. [21]. In one study, researchers administered the Yale-Brown Obsessive Compulsive Scale (Y-BOCS) symptom checklist [22] to 343 Japanese patients with OCD to examine whether the symptom dimensions were stable across cultures [23]. They found that the OCD symptom structure has substantial transcultural stability across Western and Eastern cultures, suggesting that OCD is mediated by universal psychobiological mechanisms.

FEAR OF CONTAMINATION IN OCD

The fear of contamination (e.g., "I avoid using public toilets because I am afraid of disease or contamination") features prominently in approximately half of all cases of OCD [24]. Typical examples of perceived pollutants are:

Bodily excretions (urine, feces)
Bodily fluids (sweat, saliva, mucus, tears, etc.)
Blood
Semen
Garbage
Household chemicals
Radioactivity
Spoiled food
Lead
Asbestos
Pets
Birds
Dead animals
Factories and construction sites

Fear of Contamination in Obsessive-Compulsive Disorder 13

Infectious contaminants include bodily products such as blood, hospitals, and people/places thought to be associated with infectious contaminants. Most sufferers experience intense compulsions when faced with these contaminants (or thoughts of them) to reduce their chances of contamination. Compulsions include any protective act that an individual carries out to avoid becoming contaminated or to remove contamination that has somehow already occurred. Compulsions and avoidance behavior of this type may include:

Excessive and sometimes ritualized hand washing
Disinfecting or sterilizing objects/food
Throwing objects/food away unnecessarily
Frequently changing clothes
Creating clean areas that are off-limits to others
Avoiding going to certain places or touching certain objects

Some people with OCD engage in reassurance-seeking behaviors. This form of compulsion can include double-checking to make sure that they have not become contaminated or asking others for reassurance that they have not. Sufferers will sometimes repeatedly ask others to check parts of their bodies they cannot reach or see or objects they cannot go near.

Table 1. Comparison between obsessive-compulsive disorder and "neat freaks"

OCD	Neat freaks
The behavior interferes with living their life.	The behavior does not interfere with living their life.
The person cannot control his or her behavior.	The person can control his or her behavior and decides to not engage in rituals by his/herself.
The person believes that dirt has terrible effects or brings disaster to his/herself and family.	The person does not think that dirt has terrible effects or brings disaster to his/herself and family.
The person is uneasy about and afraid of invisible dirt.	The person is not uneasy about or afraid of invisible dirt.
If someone with dirty hands touches an object, a patient with OCD feels that the dirt will spread to other, surrounding, objects.	If someone with dirty hands touches something, a "neat freak" does not feel that the dirt will spread to other things, as long as the dirt is invisible.

It must be said that, sometimes, people who like things clean are just people who like things clean. This book is focusing on the extreme, pathological need for neatness that is a subset of OCD. "Neat freaks" are often mislabeled as having OCD. So what is the difference? Do all people with OCD engage in excessive cleanliness? The differences between the two are summarized in Table 1.

OCD ASSESSMENT TOOLS

Yale-Brown Obsessive Compulsive Scale (Y-BOCS)

Several assessment tools have been developed that evaluate the severity of OCD symptoms in the Japanese population. In particular, the Y-BOCS [22] [25] is one of the most commonly used scales in OCD research. This scale uses a semi-structured interview format, consisting of 10 core items that assess time spent on obsessions/compulsions, resistance to compulsions, degree of interference obsessions/compulsions with everyday life, distress generated by the obsessions/compulsions, and control over obsessions/compulsions [22][25]. The Y-BOCS yields three severity scores: obsessions, compulsions, and an overall score. Furthermore, it possesses a 67-item symptom checklist that allows for an accurate assessment of symptoms. This scale has excellent psychometric properties and is useful in research on treatment outcomes [26] [28]. However, it has three notable limitations that prevent it from being appropriate for clinical settings. First, due to its interview-based format, it can be time-consuming and expensive to administer—that is, it requires trained interviewers, and interviewer reliability must be established to ensure accurate results. Second, the 10 core items do not contain information on the specific content of the obsessions and compulsions. Although this information can be obtained from the symptom checklist, this checklist has such a large number of items that it is not effective for quickly identifying the nature and severity of patients' symptoms in actual practice [27]. Third, the Y-BOCS symptom checklist includes a list of subtypes assessed using a dichotomous (yes/no) rating scale, which means that it is unable to provide a continuous measure of OCD symptom dimensions. Therefore, Y-BOCS scores are weakly influenced by the subtypes of OCD, which makes it an inappropriate tool for clinical settings because it is unable to capture the range of severities of certain subtypes, which would affect how it is treated.

A self-report version of the Y-BOCS was created by Baer [29]. Respondents are asked to report to what extent they have experience with items such as "I have violent or horrific images in my mind" or "I am concerned by dirt or germs." A Japanese version of the self-report Y-BOCS has been developed by Hamagaki, Takagi, Urushihara, Ishisaka, and Matumoto [30]. However, the symptom checklist of the self-report Y-BOCS is somewhat problematic, in that the validity of the assignment of symptoms to categories is questionable, the self-report format might be inadequate in distinguishing between those with clinical OCD and those without OCD, and there are some issues with the wording of the items [31-32].

Maudsley Obsessive-Compulsive Inventory

The Maudsley Obsessive-Compulsive Inventory (MOCI) is a self-report measure consisting of 30 true/false items [33-35]; both the original and the Japanese version (the MOCI-J) have satisfactory test-retest reliability and internal consistency [33-35]. Factor analysis has revealed four subscales: Cleaning, Checking, Slowness, and Doubting [33]. However, the MOCI has two notable limitations [27-28]. First, the dichotomous true/false format makes the scale insensitive overall, as it can only assess the severity of specific symptoms, and it may only be effective in assessing changes in severity post-treatment. Second, the MOCI-J does not provide an adequate assessment of obsessional rumination [37]. In addition, this scale primarily assesses compulsive rituals and overemphasizes the Cleaning and Checking rituals to the exclusion of other types of neutralizing activities [28].

Padua Inventory

The Padua Inventory [38] contains 60 items, each rated on a 0–5 scale, that assess common obsessions and behavioral compulsions. The Padua Inventory has four factors: Impaired Mental Control, Contamination, Checking, and Loss of Control of Actions [38]. The questionnaire has adequate internal consistency, test-retest reliability, and discriminant validity [28] [38]. A Japanese version of the Padua Inventory was developed by Sugiura and Tanno [39]. However, this instrument has difficulty in differentiating between obsession and worry [40]. Furthermore, the Padua

Inventory does not include some categories of obsessions and compulsions, such as neutralizing and hoarding [27] [41].

Obsessive-Compulsive Inventory

The Obsessive-Compulsive Inventory (OCI) is another self-report scale for measuring OC symptoms [27]. This scale has 42 items (e.g., "I avoid using public toilets because I am afraid of disease or contamination"), each of which is rated on a five-point Likert scale corresponding to the frequency and distress of OC symptoms in the past month and severity of distress (e.g., 0 = "not at all distressed" to 4 = "extremely distressed"). The full scale yields a total possible score of 168. We believe that the OCI is a more advantageous measurement than are the other scales discussed for three reasons. First, the OCI is a more comprehensive instrument than the Y-BOCS, MOCI, or Padua Inventory because it contains seven subscales, which allows it to capture the considerable heterogeneity of obsessions and compulsions [27]. These subscales include Washing (eight items), Checking (nine items), Mental Neutralizing (six items), Obsessing (eight items), Ordering (five items), Hoarding (three items), and Doubting (three items). In addition, unlike the Y-BOCS, administration of the OCI does not require trained interviewers. Therefore, the OCI covers a wide range of OC phenomena in a format that is easy to administer and can be used to assess not only obsessions and compulsions in groups with diagnosable OCD, but also OC thoughts and behaviors in the general population [27][42]. Foa et al. [27] reported good to excellent internal consistency for both the full scale and the subscales for patients with OCD, and found that the scale had good to excellent test-retest reliability for OCD patients across two weeks. The OCI also demonstrates excellent discriminant validity because OCD patients reported greater distress on the OCI than did other-anxious controls (i.e., people with posttraumatic stress disorder or generalized social phobia). Finally, because the OCI total scores were positively associated with the total scores of the MOCI, the OCI was shown to have satisfactory convergent validity [27]. The psychometric properties of the OCI and its subscales have also been examined in a non-clinical student sample [42], which indicated a high internal consistency and good test-retest reliability for the total scale and each subscale. Simonds et al. [42] also found that the OCI had good convergent validity with the MOCI.

Our research team developed a Japanese version of the OCI (OCI-J), and validated it in both non-clinical and clinical Japanese populations [43]. In this study, the OCI-J, the MOCI, and measures of anxiety and depression were administered to 150 undergraduate students (the non-clinical sample) to investigate the internal consistency and convergent validity of the OCI-J. Correlational analysis indicated moderate to high correlations between the subscales and total scores of the OCI-J and MOCI. Furthermore, 118 non-clinical participants completed the OCI-J after a 2-week interval to determine the test-retest reliability. The OCI-J and its subscales demonstrated satisfactory test-retest reliabilities. Finally, OCD participants (n = 35), anxiety control participants with panic disorder (n = 22), and healthy control participants (n = 37) completed the OCI-J to test its clinical discrimination ability. As predicted, participants with OCD had significantly higher mean scores on OCI-J than the anxious and healthy controls. This result demonstrated that the OCI-J showed good clinical discrimination between patients with OCD and healthy and anxiety control groups. Thus, the OCI-J is a valid and reliable instrument for measuring OCD symptoms in both clinical and non-clinical samples in the Japanese population.

COGNITIVE THEORY OF OCD

Cognitive models of anxiety disorders emphasize the key role of cognitive appraisals in increasing the subjective sense of anxiety, which in turn motivates safety-seeking behaviors [44-49]. For example, cognitive appraisals focusing on the fear of physical harm (e.g., "I fear that I will get seriously ill"), mental harm (e.g., "I fear that I will lose control of my mind"), or social harm (e.g., "I fear that I will be rejected by other people") can result in the fear of contamination and an urge to wash [47].

Prior to the growth of cognitive clinical psychology, patients' beliefs and cognitions about their disorder were not specific targets of clinical assessment. The aim of the clinical assessment was to collect information that would enable the therapist to form a case formulation and treatment plan. Rachman [47] pointed out a number of beliefs and appraisals concerning fear of contamination (e.g., To avoid illness, I must always handle garbage and garbage bins very carefully; I wash my hands after handling money because it's so dirty; I'm sure to contract an illness whenever I travel; I avoid public telephones because they are sources of contamination; I worry that I might pick up a contamination that will affect my health years from now; Once contaminated, always contaminated—it doesn't go away).

IMAGERY IN FEAR OF CONTAMINATION

Imagery in OCD may be particularly relevant for people who report contamination fears; indeed, a recent cognitive behavioral theory of contamination has suggested that feelings of dirtiness and urges to wash can be evoked by internal events such as imagery [47]. Coughtrey, Shafran, and Rachman [54] developed a questionnaire to assess imagery associated with contamination fears (the Mental Contamination Imagery Questionnaire [MCIQ]). The questionnaire was designed to capture a wide range of dimensions of imagery and included items to assess image vividness ("I have very vivid, clear, images of being dirty or contaminated"), ease of dismissal ("I find it very hard to get rid of pictures of dirt and contamination'), urge to wash ("Some pictures in my mind make me want to wash"), imagery perspective ("I picture dirt and contamination through my own eyes, as if I'm actually there" and "I picture dirt and contamination as if I'm watching a film of myself') and associated distress ("I find having pictures of dirt and contamination in my mind extremely distressing"). The results of the questionnaire study, which used both clinical and non-clinical samples, indicated that compared to non-clinical participants, people with contamination-OCD reported images associated with contamination that were more vivid, harder to dismiss, and more distressing. In conclusion, Coughtrey et al. [54] suggested that assessing and addressing imagery in therapy for contamination fears may be beneficial to reducing said fears. With further development, the MCIQ may be a useful tool for clinicians to quickly assess the presence of imagery related to contamination. This would be important because these images can maintain contamination fears and compulsive washing behavior.

INFLATED SENSE OF RESPONSIBILITY

Salkovskis [49] [53] proposed that an inflated sense of responsibility for harm to oneself or others (e.g., "I often feel responsible for things that go wrong") might be connected to unwanted intrusive thoughts (including images and/or impulses) and compulsions. *Responsibility interpretation* was found to lead to both adverse mood (anxiety and depression) and the motivation and decision to engage in neutralizing behaviors (e.g., compulsive checking, washing, and covert ritualizing). In OCD, the occurrence and content of intrusions (thoughts, images, impulses, doubts) are interpreted as indicating that the person may be responsible for harm to themselves or others. In addition, *responsibility attitudes* are the origin of specific negative appraisals. Such assumptions often form as adaptive ways of coping with early experiences, but may trigger OCD when activated by critical incidents. The assumption of responsibility increases the likelihood that individuals will react to intrusions with a responsibility interpretation, which in turn increases the likelihood of engaging in behaviors that they believe will diminish the risk of causing harm, either by action or inaction.

The Responsibility Attitude Scale (RAS) and the Responsibility Interpretation Questionnaire (RIQ) were designed to evaluate the extent and specificity of responsibility assumptions and appraisals [53]. Ishikawa, Kobori, Ikota, and Shimizu [50] developed Japanese versions of the RAS (RAS-J; e.g., *I often feel responsible for things which go wrong*; *I am too sensitive to feeling responsible for things going wrong*) and RIQ (RIQ-J; e.g., *I could be responsible for serious harm*; *I cannot take the risk of this thought coming true*). They indicated that both scales about responsibility were related to the severity of obsessive-compulsive symptoms using Japanese sample. In the study by Ishikawa et al. [50], participants were 118 non-clinical Japanese students who completed the RAS-J and RIQ-J to confirm the test-retest reliability of the scales. Ishikawa et al. [50] recruited a sample of 98 participants (OCD group: $n = 37$; anxiety control group: $n = 24$; healthy control group: $n = 37$). Potential OCD participants ($n = 37$) were diagnosed by a psychiatrist using the OCD criteria of the Diagnostic and Statistical Manual of Mental Disorders, 4th edition, Text Revision (DSM-IV-TR, American Psychiatric Association). Individuals were excluded if they had a comorbid disorder on Axis I or II of the DSM-IV-TR (e.g., another anxiety disorder, major depression, mental retardation, a personality or psychotic disorder, dementia, or substance use disorder). Potential anxiety control participants ($n = 24$) were diagnosed by a psychiatrist using the DSM-IV-TR criteria for panic disorder. Anxiety control individuals were excluded if they had a comorbid Axis I or II disorder, but not if they had a comorbid anxiety disorder other than OCD (e.g., a patient with panic disorder and social anxiety disorder). The frequency of each principal anxiety disorder was as follows: panic disorder without agoraphobia, 50%; panic disorder with agoraphobia, 32%; panic disorder without agoraphobia and comorbid general anxiety disorder, 9%; panic disorder with agoraphobia and comorbid social anxiety disorder, 5%; and panic disorder with agoraphobia and comorbid PTSD, 5%. Finally, non-clinical participants were Japanese university students. Potential participants

($n = 37$) were excluded if they reported a clinical history of mental disorder, head injury, central nervous system diseases, or substance abuse. All participants completed the RAS-J, RIQ-J, and other measures to assess the validity of the RAS-J and RIQ-J. Analyses showed that the RAS-J and RIQ-J had adequate test-retest reliability and internal consistency. In addition, both scales had adequate concurrent validity, demonstrated by significant correlations with other measures of OCD, anxiety, and depression. Group comparisons using ANOVAs with the Bonferroni correction indicated that the RAS-J and RIQ-J scores of the OCD group not only differed from the non-clinical group, but also from the clinically anxious comparison group. The study demonstrated that the newly developed RAS-J and RIQ-J effectively measure responsibility attitudes and interpretations in Japanese patients with OCD. The results also support the hypothesis that, among Japanese people with OCD, appraisals of responsibility for causing or preventing harm are important because they lead to discomfort and motivate attempts to neutralize intrusions [48] [51] [52]. These findings have implications for clinical work, especially in CBT with obsessive-compulsive clients [28][49]. For example, measures of responsibility could be used as outcome measures to assess the effectiveness of CBT for OCD.

CONCLUSION

OCD affects roughly 1%–2.5% of the general population. Several assessment tools have been developed that evaluate the severity of OCD symptoms, such as Y-BOCS and OCI. Cognitive models of anxiety disorders emphasize the key role of cognitive appraisals in increasing the subjective sense of anxiety, which in turn motivates OCD. For example, cognitive appraisals focusing on the fear of physical harm, mental harm, or social harm can result in the fear of contamination and an urge to wash. In addition, an inflated sense of responsibility for harm to oneself or others might be connected to unwanted intrusive thoughts (including images and/or impulses) and compulsions.

Chapter 3

MENTAL CONTAMINATION

ABSTRACT

Mental contamination is an internal, emotional feeling of dirtiness that may be evoked by unwanted thoughts and images, as well as by memories of negative events, such as sexual assaults. Mental contamination is primarily caused by experiences involving humans (e.g., violators or perpetrators) as opposed to substances (e.g., dirt or bodily fluids). For example, feelings of mental contamination may develop following experiences of ill treatment, sexual assault, domination, degradation, manipulation, betrayal, or humiliation. A study showed that 46% of participants with obsessive-compulsive symptoms experienced mental contamination, and the severity was positively associated with the severity of their OCD symptoms.

INTRODUCTION

Kegare is a Japanese concept that means a type of personal "impurity." This concept dates back to ancient times in Japan, when it was widely used. The notion of *kegare* is unique to Japan and has heavily influenced Japanese culture, philosophy, history, religion, and personalities. A ban or an inhibition resulting from a social custom or emotional aversion is called an immorality. In ancient Japan, *kegare* was an abominable immorality, and Japanese people would often make every possible effort to avoid such immoral activities. They had to avoid *kegare* to maintain their cleanliness and purity. In Japanese religion, there was great aversion to the state of *kegare,* which could be associated with evil or even death. Therefore, a person who carried *kegare* was forbidden to enter sacred places, such as shrines and the Imperial Palace. *Kegare* was regarded as tangible, and the process of removing it was known as *harai*. *Kegare* could be washed off with clean water, a special *harai* process known as *misogi* (which means "to purify with water"). Despite the tangibility of *kegare*, the distinction between guilt and *kegare* was vague in ancient Japan. In Japanese traditional religion, sin and *kegare* were seen as equivalent. In fact, sometimes *kegare* is referred to as "*sin-kegare.*" In ancient times, a person who committed a political crime was considered to be affected by *kegare* and was ousted from the town. The concept of impurity appears to have been common in many primitive societies. These perspectives may influence our culture, philosophy, history, religion, behavior, and personality.

Table 2. Differences between mental contamination and an ordinary sense of dirtiness

Ordinary sense of dirtiness (i.e., contact contamination)	Mental contamination
Feelings of dirtiness that are evoked by physical contact with soiled substance/material/person	Feelings of dirtiness that are evoked with or without physical contact with soiled substance/material/person
Cannot be evoked by memories, repugnant thoughts or images. Rarely revived by memories, repugnant thoughts or images	The feelings of dirtiness can be evoked or revived by memories, repugnant thoughts and/or images
Generally responsive to cleaning of the site of the dirtiness/contamination. The feeling of dirtiness can be fully alleviated by cleaning	The feelings of dirtiness are not properly responsive to cleaning
Often accompanied by revulsion and disgust. Occasionally accompanied by anxiety and/or distress. Rarely accompanied by guilt or shame.	The feelings of dirtiness are accompanied by negative emotions that may include revulsion, disgust, shame, guilt, anxiety, and distress
The bodily location of the dirt/contamination is readily identifiable	Bodily location of feelings of dirtiness is not readily identifiable
The feelings of dirtiness generate an urge to clean	The feelings of dirtiness generate an urge to clean
Resolves promptly following attempts at alleviation	Often persists despite attempts at alleviation

MENTAL CONTAMINATION

In clinical psychology, some researchers have suggested a different type of contamination—one that is experienced without physical contact [46] [47] [55]. This phenomenon, first identified by Rachman [56], is called "mental pollution" This psychological sense of contamination involves an internal, emotional feeling of dirtiness that may be evoked by unwanted thoughts and images, as well as by memories of negative events, such as sexual assaults. Fairbrother and Rachman [55] described several key differences between mental contamination and the feeling of dirtiness and contamination induced by contact with soiled substances or objects (i.e., an ordinary sense of dirtiness). These differences are summarized in Table 2.

Rachman suggested that "mental contamination has a long past, but a short history" [47]. Indeed, the term "pollution of the mind" was introduced by John Bunyan in the 15th century to explain his reaction to intrusive blasphemous thoughts, but was ignored until relatively recently [47] [57]. Mental contamination is primarily caused by experiences involving humans (e.g., violators or perpetrators) as opposed to substances (e.g., dirt or bodily fluids). For example, feelings of mental contamination may develop following experiences of ill treatment, sexual assault, domination, degradation, manipulation, betrayal, or humiliation [47]. Many researchers have found that thoughts related to sexual trauma are particularly strong predictors of mental contamination [55] [63-65] (see, Chapter 4). Rachman, Radomsky, Elliott, and Zysk [58] reported that introducing the element of betrayal boosts the magnitude of mental contamination. They also demonstrated that mental contamination can be provoked in some perpetrators of non-consensual acts involving betrayal (e.g., the betrayal of a close friend and his anxious, shy little sister by kissing the sister against her will when asked to look after her). In addition, threats to one's moral purity can also lead to a sense of moral threat, which may provoke a perceived need for physical cleansing. For instance, Zhong and Liljenquist [59] demonstrated that non-clinical participants who were asked to copy an unethical story (e.g., sabotaging a co-worker) showed an increased desire for cleansing products (e.g., shower, soap) as compared to participants asked to copy an ethical story. Furthermore, they showed that physical cleansing reduces perceived threats to one's moral self-image, suggesting that physical cleansing may be used as a way of "washing away" moral sins through symbolic self-completion.

The sense of mental contamination is thought to be common. A study conducted by Coughtrey, Shafran, Knibbs, and Rachman [60] examined the sense of mental contamination in OCD. Participants ($n = 177$) with obsessive-compulsive symptoms were assessed for mental contamination. The analyses showed that 46% of participants experienced mental contamination, and the severity was positively associated with the severity of their OCD symptoms. Of the total sample, 10.2% reported mental contamination without clinically relevant contact contamination (i.e., an ordinary sense of dirtiness), 15.3% reported contact contamination without clinically relevant mental contamination, 36.1% experienced both mental and contact contamination, and 38.5% did not report any contamination fears.

MENTAL CONTAMINATION IN CHILDHOOD SEXUAL ABUSE

Studied have demonstrated that many survivors of childhood sexual abuse suffer from mental contamination for years or decades after the abuse. For example, children may feel disgusted when touching or looking at their own bodies, or worry that others can see that they have been victimized. Some studies of PTSD have examined this distressing symptom [11] [47] [74] [75]. Berman, Wheaton, Fabricant, and Abramowitz [65] examined whether mental contamination would be associated with four factors as in previous literature: (1) Christian religiosity, (2) intrinsic motivation toward the Christian religion, (3) parental guilt induction (e.g., emotional abuse), and (4) childhood trauma. Their study indicated that mental contamination was not associated with the degree of religiosity, yet it was positively associated with exposure to childhood trauma and maladaptive guilt-induction strategies by one's parents (emotional abuse). They found that childhood trauma was also positively associated with feelings of mental contamination. They discussed that this relationship might be explained by the repeated internalization of emotionally hurtful remarks. Given that emotional abuse tends to involve repeated statements or behaviors that target the victim's self-worth or sense of self (e.g., insults, verbal assaults, name calling, feeling hated by the family), the child victim might internalize the abuse and come to view the comments or behaviors as an accurate reflection of him or herself as intrinsically disgusting or worthless, which in turn leads to feelings of contamination. Thus, Berman et al. [65] suggested that clinicians should assess patients for possible childhood trauma (specifically emotional and sexual abuse), and inquire about exposure to parenting strategies that involved maladaptive guilt induction (e.g., blaming the child for negative outcomes when he/she was not at fault).

FEAR OF MORPHING

People with mental contamination may experience a fear of morphing, or "transformation obsessions" [61], whereby they are afraid that they may take on the undesirable characteristics of an unsavory person and, in extreme cases, turn into them. The type of person classified as undesirable is both personally and culturally defined, but may include personal enemies or people who are considered weird, dirty, or of low status [47]. Beliefs about morphing may be particularly associated with issues of self-identity. Therefore, cognitive behavioral therapy (CBT) sessions might include behavioral experiments to reinforce patients' self-identity, increase self-esteem, and thus reduce their vulnerability to morphing fears (e.g., making a list of personal characteristics that are stable and unchanging) [78]. For example, Coughtrey, Shafran, Lee and Rachman [78] reported on an OCD patient who suffered from morphing. In this case series, the patient was vulnerable to a sense of morphing into people she interpreted as undesirable, or that her loved ones disliked or pitied (e.g., obese people or alcoholics). The patient described noticing magical omens relating to her fear of morphing. She cleaned herself and her clothes if she came into contact with the people who were the targets of her fear of morphing. The authors demonstrated that addressing self-esteem and the stability of self-concept was important for patients with fear of morphing. They considered self-esteem particularly important in cases of mental contamination to increase the stability of the sense of self, as this appeared to contribute to some participants' feelings of vulnerability to morphing.

CONCLUSION

Mental contamination is an internal, emotional feeling of dirtiness that may be evoked by unwanted thoughts and images, as well as by memories of negative events, such as sexual assaults. For example, the feelings of dirtiness can be evoked or revived by memories, repugnant thoughts and/or images. Introducing the element of betrayal boosts the magnitude of mental contamination. Studies have demonstrated that many survivors of childhood sexual abuse suffer from mental contamination for years or decades after the abuse. People with mental contamination may experience a fear of morphing, or transformation obsessions.

Chapter 4

SEXUAL ASSAULT AND MENTAL CONTAMINATION

ABSTRACT

Thoughts related to sexual trauma are particularly strong predictors of mental contamination. Ishikawa, Kobori, and Shimizu [62] investigated how unwanted sexual experiences can evoke mental contamination. In this study, 148 female participants was asked to recall their most distressing unwanted sexual experiences. Indices of mental contamination were then assessed. The findings of this study indicated that mental contamination can be caused by deliberately remembering an unwanted sexual experience. The study also showed that feelings of dirtiness can be provoked by deliberately remembering unwanted sexual experiences, including forms that entail no physical contact (i.e., verbal and visual sexual assault). Furthermore, the study presented new findings that the degree of mental contamination differs depending on the type of sexual assault.

INTRODUCTION

Some studies have reported that thoughts related to sexual trauma are particularly strong predictors of mental contamination [55] [63-65]. For example, Fairbrother and Rachman [55] found that 60% of a sample of non-clinical female participants who had experienced sexual assault at least 3 months before being interviewed reported at least one symptom of mental contamination when they deliberately recalled the sexual assault. They also showed that the severity of mental contamination was related to the severity of PTSD. This chapter demonstrates how unwanted sexual experiences can evoke mental contamination.

TYPES OF SEXUAL ASSAULTS

The criteria employed to classify an event as a sexual assault or an unwanted sexual experience varies across studies [66]. The U.S. Department of Health and Human Services [1] indicated that unwanted sexual experiences can indeed be verbal or visual—anything that forces a person into unwanted sexual contact or attention. This includes victims of voyeurism (being watched by someone else while naked or engaging in private sexual acts) and exhibitionism (being forced to see someone else's genitals or sexual act). "Rape" is defined as being physically forced or psychologically coerced into engaging in vaginal, anal, or oral penetration by one or more persons or by a foreign object. In contrast, sexual assault includes a wide range of victimizations (e.g., grabbing, fondling, and verbal threats), separate from rape/attempted rape [67]. In Japan, Sasagawa et al. [3] investigated the statistics on unwanted sexual experiences among 946 Japanese women, classifying the unwanted sexual experiences that Japanese women often encounter into four main categories:

(a) Verbal sexual assault: being abused or harassed verbally;
(b) Visual sexual assault: being forced to look at a sexual object;
(c) Forcible touching/frottage: forced touching, fondling or grabbing of any part of one's body (e.g. sexual organs, buttocks, breast, or mouth); being forced to touch the offender's body;
(d) Rape/attempted rape: forced engagement in sexual intercourse; vaginal, anal, or oral penetration by the offender. These criteria include threats and attempts at rape that were not carried out, but which involved some physical contact (e.g. being made to take off one's clothes or being pushed onto a bed).

Note that (a) and (b) do not involve physical contact, while (c) and (d) do involve physical contact.

UNWANTED SEXUAL EXPERIENCES THAT EVOKE MENTAL CONTAMINATION

Ishikawa, Kobori, and Shimizu [62] investigated how unwanted sexual experiences can evoke mental contamination. If clinicians understand this process, they will be better able to identify patients who are at risk for mental contamination and deliver appropriate treatments to victims who have experienced types of sexual assault associated with a high risk of mental contamination. For this purpose, non-clinical female participants were asked to remember their most distressing unwanted sexual experiences.

METHOD

Participants in the study were 257 Japanese female undergraduates (age range: 18–28 years; $M = 18.45$, $SD = 1.51$). Among them, 148 reported one or more unwanted sexual experience, such as (a) verbal sexual assault, (b) visual sexual assault, (c) forcible touching/frottage, or (d) rape/attempted rape.

In the study, dependent variables were indices of mental contamination, including a feeling of dirtiness, an urge to wash, internal negative emotions (INEs), and external negative emotions (ENEs). These four indices of mental contamination were assessed both before and after the recall of their most disturbing unwanted sexual assault using the Mental Contamination Report (MCR) [94]. The MCR uses subjective units of distress (SUDs) to assess feelings of dirtiness (one item); the urge to wash (five items on rinsing the mouth, brushing the teeth, washing the face, washing the hands, and taking a shower); INEs (seven items regarding shame, guilt, humiliation, fear, sadness, and self-perception as cheap and sleazy); and ENEs (five items regarding anxiety, distress, anger, and disgust towards the offender's physical appearance or behavior). A sample item is presented below (Figure 1), along with the procedure of the study.

Figure 1. Sample item from the MCR.

(1) First, all participants were asked to complete the MCR (pre-recall MCR).

(2) In order to induce mental contamination, participants who had had one or more unwanted sexual experiences were asked to recall what had happened, and to describe only their most distressing experience (no additional unwanted sexual experiences) on the questionnaire, in 100 words or less. Participants who had never had an unwanted sexual experience were not required to do anything else after filling out the questionnaire. These participants took only the pre-recall MCR and were thanked for their participation.

(3) Participants were then asked to classify their most distressing unwanted sexual experience into one of four categories: verbal sexual assault, visual sexual assault, forcible touching/frottage, or rape/attempted rape. These four categories were based on those identified by Sasagawa et al. [3], as these were found to be typical of unwanted sexual experiences among Japanese women.

(4) After participants had recalled and described their most distressing unwanted sexual experience, they took the MCR again (post-recall MCR).

(5) Participants who had recalled their most distressing unwanted sexual experience were asked to complete the Impact of Event Scale – Revised (IES-R) to assess PTSD symptoms. The IES-R has 22 questions and is based on the DSM-IV criteria for PTSD [69]. The IES-R asks about intrusive thoughts, nightmares, intrusive feelings and imagery, dissociative-like re-experiencing of traumatic events, avoidance, and hyperarousal. We used the Japanese version of the IES-R (IES-R-J), which was developed and validated by Asukai et al. [70]. In order to measure PTSD symptoms specifically stemming from each distinct type of unwanted sexual experience, participants were asked to complete this questionnaire with reference to their memories of within one month after the occurrence of the traumatic event.

After completing the last step of the study, all participants were fully debriefed about the study's goals and mental contamination, and were thanked for participating. All participants were urged to contact the researcher if they experienced any distress following their participation in the study, and were informed that the researcher could refer them to sources of support.

RESULT

The results showed that of the 148 females who reported their most distressing unwanted sexual experience, 24 reported verbal sexual assault, 22 reported visual sexual assault, 86 reported forcible touching/frottage, and 16 reported rape/attempted rape. Participants' scores for feelings of dirtiness were based on responses to one item on the MCR. Scores for the urge to wash were based on the average of five items ($\alpha = 0.80$). Scores for INEs (e.g., shame and guilt) were calculated as the average of seven items on the MCR ($\alpha = 0.78$), while scores for ENEs (e.g., anxiety, distress) were based on the average of five items ($\alpha = 0.81$). The means and standard deviations for the indices of mental contamination are shown in Table 3.

Table 3. Mean scores and standard deviations for indices of mental contamination

	Verbal sexual assault (N=24)		Visual sexual assault (N=22)		Forcible touching/frottage (N=86)		Rape/attempted rape (N=16)	
	Pre	Post	Pre	Post	Pre	Post	Pre	Post
Dirtiness	13.79	24.58	20.73	32.73	18.12	31.51	20.00	61.31
	(16.57)	(28.73)	(13.78)	(21.68)	(11.44)	(27.60)	(19.15)	(21.70)
Washing–urge	31.47	33.04	33.14	34.53	31.92	33.02	26.71	34.69
	(22.24)	(25.99)	(28.31)	(26.61)	(21.54)	(21.91)	(12.06)	(22.49)
INE	16.46	26.96	14.05	31.46	14.04	26.31	13.10	34.40
	(14.70)	(22.83)	(5.66)	(26.05)	(13.95)	(21.75)	(19.80)	(24.11)
ENE	22.55	43.39	21.01	39.17	21.61	44.81	23.38	39.32
	(15.75)	(28.40)	(18.96)	(32.08)	(17.30)	(27.28)	(23.01)	(29.80)
IES-R-J	26.08 (17.00)		21.50 (22.93)		25.07 (16.70)		42.75 (23.46)	

To evaluate the effects of remembering the most disturbing unwanted sexual experience on symptoms, we conducted a 2 (time: pre and post recall) × 4 (group: verbal sexual assault, visual sexual assault, forcible touching/frottage, and rape/attempted rape) repeated measures multivariate analysis of variance (MANOVA) with the feeling of dirtiness, urge to wash, INEs, and ENEs as the four dependent variables. The results showed a significant group effect ($F[12, 429] = 1.96$, $p < .05$), time effect ($F[4, 141] = 22.08$, $p < .001$), and group × time interaction ($F[12, 429] = 3.03$, $p < .001$).

Follow-up analyses of the repeated-measures ANOVAs were then carried out, followed by multiple comparisons using the Bonferroni correction. The analyses were conducted with time (before and after recall) as a within-subjects factor and the four groups (verbal sexual assault, visual sexual assault, forcible touching/frottage, and rape/attempted rape) as a between-subjects factor, with feelings of dirtiness, the urge to wash, INEs, and ENEs as dependent variables.

With feelings of dirtiness as the dependent variable, the main effects of time (F [1, 144] = 50.13, $p < .001$, $\eta_p^2 = .26$), group (F [3, 144] = 3.60, $p = .02$, $\eta_p^2 = .07$), and the interaction between time and group (F [3, 144] = 5.31, $p = .01$, $\eta_p^2 = .10$) were all significant. Post-hoc simple main effect analyses were guided based on data exploration. These post-hoc analyses for time revealed significant differences between pre-recall and post-recall scores in the verbal sexual assault ($p = .05$), visual sexual assault ($p = .04$), forcible touching/frottage ($p < .001$), and rape/attempted rape ($p < .001$) groups. Simple main effect analyses for group revealed that the post-recall scores for the rape/attempted rape group differed significantly from those of the verbal sexual assault ($p < .001$), visual sexual assault ($p = .01$), and forcible touching/frottage ($p < .001$) groups. This result suggests that mental contamination increased in all groups that recalled unwanted sexual experiences; however, the rape/attempted rape group reported the highest levels of post-recall feelings of dirtiness (see Figure 2).

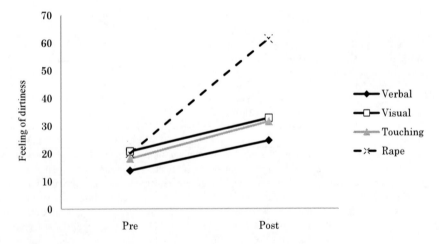

Figure 2. Pre- and post-recall scores for the feeling of dirtiness.

With the urge to wash as the dependent variable, the interaction between time and group was significant (F [3, 144] = 2.79, $p = .03$, $\eta_p^2 = .07$). Post-hoc simple main effect analyses revealed a significant difference between pre-recall and post-recall scores only in the rape/attempted rape group ($p = .02$). This result indicates that only the rape/attempted rape group reported a stronger urge to wash at post-recall, while all other groups experienced no change in the urge to wash after recalling their experiences (see Figure 3).

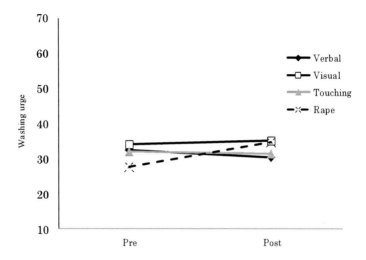

Figure 3. Pre- and post-recall scores for the urge to wash.

With INEs as the dependent variable, the main effect for time was significant ($F[1, 144] = 60.42, p < .001, \eta_p^2 = .30$). Likewise, with ENEs as the dependent variable, the main effect for time was also significant ($F[1, 144] = 49.12, p < .001, \eta_p^2 = .26$). These results indicate that recalling unwanted sexual experiences evoked both INEs and ENEs (see Figure 4 and Figure 5).

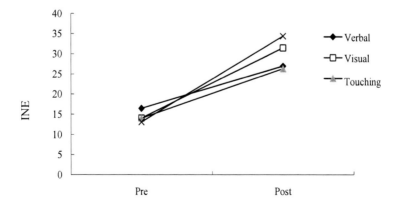

Figure 4. Pre- and post-recall scores for internal negative emotions (INEs).

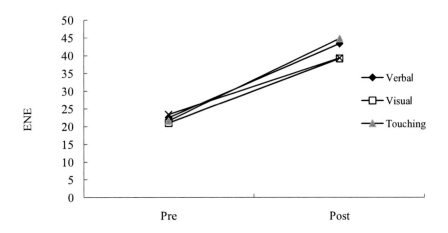

Figure 5. Pre- and post-recall scores for external negative emotion (ENEs).

DISCUSSION

The findings of this study suggest that mental contamination can be caused by deliberately remembering an unwanted sexual experience [55] [63]. The study also shows that feelings of dirtiness can be provoked by deliberately remembering unwanted sexual experiences, including forms that entail no physical contact (i.e., verbal and visual sexual assault). Furthermore, the study presented new findings that the degree of mental contamination differs depending on the type of sexual assault. Regarding the degree of feelings of dirtiness, the post-recall scores of the rape/attempted rape group were higher than were those of any other group, indicating that stronger feelings of dirtiness were evoked in victims who remembered a rape or attempted rape. Actively remembering a rape experience seems to exacerbate strong existing feelings of mental contamination. In addition, the present study demonstrated that individuals who remembered their rape/attempted rape experiences felt an urge to wash, although those remembering other types of unwanted sexual experiences did not. These findings indicate that individuals remembering unwanted sexual experiences related to rape/attempted rape felt more intense dirtiness than did individuals remembering other types of unwanted sexual experience. The urge to wash could be provoked to a significant extent only in participants remembering rape/attempted rape. Thus, this study makes a valuable contribution to existing knowledge by providing evidence that victims of rape/attempted rape are at a greater risk of more severe mental contamination than are those who had other types of unwanted sexual experiences.

Furthermore, we found that the amount of mental contamination did not differ between victims of visual sexual assault, verbal sexual assault, and forcible touching. This result indicates that victims of visual or verbal sexual assault, which do not entail direct contact, might suffer mental contamination to the same degree as victims of forcible touching, which involves direct contact with the offender; however, victims of rape seem to experience stronger mental contamination than do the other three groups.

The confirmation that remembering unwanted sexual experiences can provoke mental contamination means that individuals who often remember or ruminate on such unwanted experiences in their daily lives may be at greater risk of mental contamination. For example, Conway, Mendelson, Giannopoulos, Csank, and Holm [71] that individuals who experienced sexual abuse are more likely to report negative rumination. Furthermore, the severity of PTSD has been found to be significantly correlated with the degree of rumination on the traumatic event, while rumination strengthens associations between the cognitive and emotional factors of memories [72-73]. In cases of mental contamination, rumination on unwanted sexual experiences may intensify mental contamination while also increasing depressive affect. We are investigating the relationship between mental contamination and ruminative thinking in instances of sexual assault to learn more about this effect.

CONCLUSION

Some findings evidenced that mental contamination can be caused by deliberately remembering an unwanted sexual experience. Our research team indicated that individuals remembering unwanted sexual experiences related to rape/attempted rape felt more intense dirtiness than did individuals remembering other types of unwanted sexual experience.

Chapter 5

ASSESSMENT OF MENTAL CONTAMINATION

ABSTRACT

A number of instruments have been developed to assess mental contamination. For example, Mental Pollution Questionnaire (MPQ) measures the severity of mental contamination. Our research team conducted two studies to develop a Japanese version of the MPQ-J. In sum, factor analyses and an investigation of the test-retest reliability were conducted. The result showed that the factor structure of the MPQ-J matched the two-factor model. In terms of test-retest reliability, the MPQ-J subscale scores at the two time points were moderately and significantly correlated, confirming the reliability of the MPQ-J. In addition, correlation analyses showed that MPQ-J scores were significantly associated with the fear of contact contamination (i.e., an ordinary sense of dirtiness), depression, and inflated responsibility cognitions. These results confirmed the psychometric properties of the MPQ-J.

INTRODUCTION

A full and detailed assessment is important in order to identify all sources of contamination, both mental and contact, and to establish the degree of overlap [78]. It may be helpful to use measures of mental contamination and thought-action fusion (TAF) throughout treatment in order to track and monitor the sources and forms of mental contamination. In addition, it is advisable to ask questions about betrayal and morality, and to consider that feelings of contamination can be triggered in perpetrators as well as victims. For example, it is important to ask patients whether they have ever been betrayed, whether they have betrayed someone else, and what their emotional reaction was to that betrayal [79].

A number of instruments have been developed to assess mental contamination. This chapter explains (a) vancouver obsessional compulsive inventory—mental Contamination Scale and (b) mental pollution questionnaire (MPQ).

VANCOUVER OBSESSIONAL COMPULSIVE INVENTORY— MENTAL CONTAMINATION SCALE

The first scale, to our knowledge, to directly assess it was the Vancouver Obsessional Compulsive Inventory—Mental Contamination Scale [47]. VOCI-MC is 20-item scale to various assess aspects of mental contamination. Participants rate each item (e.g., "I often feel dirty under my skin") on a 5-point scale ranging from 0 (not at all) to 4 (very much). Radomsky, Rachman, Shafran, Coughtrey, and Barber [80] assessed the psychometric properties of the VOCI-MC in participants diagnosed with OCD ($n = 57$), an anxiety disorder other than OCD ($n = 24$) and in healthy undergraduate students ($n = 410$). Their results showed that the scale had excellent psychometric properties, including internal consistency and convergent, divergent, and discriminant validity. Further, the scale accounted for significant unique variance in OCD symptoms over and above that accounted for by depression, anxiety, traditional contact-based contamination, and OCD beliefs.

MENTAL POLLUTION QUESTIONNAIRE

Cougle, Lee, Horowitz, Wolitzky-Taylor, and Telch [81] developed the Mental Pollution Questionnaire (MPQ), which measures the severity of mental contamination. The MPQ has been shown to have adequate factorial and psychometric properties in a study conducted among 208 undergraduates [81]. It consists of 8 items assessed on a Likert scale, divided into two subscales: "Washing," which assesses the use of washing behaviors to attempt to relieve feeling of distress (e.g., "I wash my hands after doing something I feel is morally wrong"; "I wash my hands when I have an obscene thought, idea, or impulse"), and "Ideation," which assesses the sense of mental contamination (e.g., "When I recall certain events, it leaves me feeling dirty"; "For me, feeling dirty inside and feeling shameful go together"). These initial items were constructed based on Rachman's [56] original article on mental pollution. In the study, MPQ scores were significantly associated with the symptoms of OCD, anxiety, and depression, as well as cognitions theoretically related to OCD: inflated responsibility [53] and TAF [82]. In addition, the study demonstrated the good test-retest reliability of the MPQ, and concluded that the MPQ is a reliable and valid measure of mental contamination or feelings of internal dirtiness.

JAPANESE VERSION OF THE MPQ (MPQ-J)

Our team conducted two studies to develop a Japanese version of the MPQ-J [83].

a) In study 1, we developed a Japanese version of the MPQ (i.e., the MPQ-J), examined its factorial validity, and investigated its test-retest reliability.
b) In Study 2, we examined additional convergent validity of the MPQ-J, testing the hypothesis that the MPQ-J would correlate with measures of obsessive washing, anxiety symptoms, depression symptoms, morality and an inflated sense of responsibility.

Study 1

In study 1, to recruit participants for the factor analysis, information about the study was provided via handouts and oral presentations in Japanese university lecture rooms, in a group setting. Since the study aimed to develop a Japanese version of the MPQ, all participants were Japanese. Prospective participants were asked to contact the researchers to request a questionnaire. The sample for Study 1 consisted of 202 undergraduates (51.50% male) (age range: 18–23; $M = 19.15$, $SD = 0.86$). All participants completed the MPQ-J in approximately 10 min.

FACTOR STRUCTURE AND INTERNAL CONSISTENCY OF THE MPQ-J

Based on the same procedure used by Cougle et al. [81], an exploratory factor analysis was conducted to extract factors from the data of all 202 participants. Factors were extracted using the maximum-likelihood method with varimax rotation, using SPSS version 18. An exploratory factor analysis of the eight items yielded two factors with eigenvalues of greater than one. The scree plot also suggested a two-factor structure. All items displaying distinctive factor loadings above .50 on one of the two distinct factors were retained as candidate items for the MPQ-J. The rotated factor matrix and loadings for each item are presented in Table 4.

Table 4. Rotated factor matrix of the MPQ-J (Ishikawa, Kobori, & Shimizu, 2014)

	Items	Factor 1	Factor 2	Communality
1	I wash my hands when I feel guilty.	.88	.11	.79
2	I wash my hands after doing something I feel is morally wrong.	.82	.11	.68
3	I wash my hands when I have an obscene thought, idea, or impulse.	.67	.26	.52
4	I feel that I am a bad person if I do not wash my hands thoroughly.	.59	.29	.43
5	Certain thoughts or images can make me feel dirty.	.26	.80	.71
6	Sometimes I feel dirty inside.	.11	.78	.62
7	When I recall certain events, it leaves me feeling dirty.	.18	.75	.59
8	For me, feeling dirty inside and feeling shameful go together.	.16	.61	.40
	Percentage of variance explained	29.76	29.48	-

The two factors explained 59.24% of the total variance (29.76% and 29.48%, respectively). The measure of sampling adequacy was 0.82, suggesting an acceptable goodness-of-fit of the factor model (sampling adequacy has a possible range of 0–1.0, with values < 0.5 suggesting a poor fit; [84]). Factor 1 (MPQ-Washing; Items 1–4) refers to washing rituals performed in response to perceived internal dirtiness, and Factor 2 (MPQ-Ideation; Items 5–8) refers to a sense of inward contamination not connected to washing behavior. The Cronbach's α was .82 for the overall 8-item scale, and .85 and .84 for Factors 1 and 2, respectively, indicating strong internal consistency.

TEST-RETEST RELIABILITY OF THE MPQ-J

To recruit participants for the test-retest analyses, information about the study was provided via handouts and oral presentations in group settings in Japanese university lecture rooms. Participants were excluded if they were not Japanese. Prospective participants were asked to contact the researchers to request a questionnaire. A total of 121 participants completed the MPQ-J. Two weeks later, 81 of the initial 121 participants were retested. At this time, they completed the measures in the same order. Test-retest reliability estimates were based on the 81 students who took the test twice (60% male; age range: 18–27; $M = 19.81$, $SD = 1.40$). None of the participants in this study had participated in the initial study examining the factor structure of the MPQ-J. The test-retest interval was 14 days. Test-retest reliability estimates were calculated using Pearson's correlations between the first and second testing. Overall, the Pearson's correlation between the MPQ-J total scores at the two time points was .71 ($p < .001$), with .69 ($p < .001$) for the MPQ-Washing subscale and .68 ($p < .001$) for the MPQ-Ideation subscale. These results demonstrated that the MPQ-J has adequate temporal stability.

STUDY 2

We also attempted to confirm the convergent validity of the MPQ-J, testing the hypothesis that the MPQ-J would correlate with measures of obsessive washing, anxiety symptoms, depression symptoms, morality and an inflated sense of responsibility. Participant recruitment followed the same procedure as in the above study: information was provided via handouts and presentations in Japanese university lecture rooms, and prospective participants contacted the researchers for a questionnaire. Participants in Study 2 were 236 undergraduates (68.64% female, age range: 18–43; $M = 20.81$, $SD = 4.42$). All participants completed the questionnaire battery in approximately 30 min. We used the following measurement tools to investigate the convergent validity of the MPQ-J.

- ***Mental contamination.*** The 8-item version of the MPQ-J resulting from Study 1 was administered to participants.
- ***Depression.*** The Beck Depression Inventory Version 2 (BDI-II) [85] is a 21-item self-report measure designed to assess the symptoms of major depression. We used the Japanese version of the BDI-II [86]. Responses are given on a 4-point Likert scale from 1 = "not at all" to 4 = "severely."
- ***Anxiety.*** The Beck Anxiety Inventory (BAI) [87] is a 21-item multiple-choice self-report inventory used to measure anxiety symptoms (numbness, hot and cold sweats, or feelings of dread) in the past week. Responses are given on a 4-point Likert scale ranging from 1 = "not at all" to 4 = "severely."
- ***Fear of contact contamination.*** We used the Washing (OCI-Washing) subscale of the OCI [27] to measure contact contamination. The OCI is a 42-item self-report measure designed to assess the symptoms of OCD. The Washing subscale consists of eight items measuring the extent to which the participant has engaged in obsessive washing behavior due to the fear of contact contamination in recent weeks (e.g., "I find it difficult to touch rubbish or dirty things."). Responses are given on a 5-point Likert scale ranging from 0 (not at all) to 4 (extremely). The Japanese version of the OCI was developed by Ishikawa, Kobori, and Shimizu [43] (see Chapter 2 for information on its development).
- ***Personality traits.*** The Japanese version of the Substance Use Risk Profile Scale (SURPS–J) assesses four dimensions of personality (i.e., personality traits) linked to different motivations for drug use and abuse [88]. This instrument was chosen not specifically for its correlation with drug and alcohol use, but because it also assesses personality traits related to anxiety and depression with only a few items, and because it has established validity and reliability [88]. The first trait, *anxiety sensitivity* refers to the fear of symptoms of physiological arousal, such as feeling dizzy [89]. The second trait, *hopelessness*, is an identified risk factor for developing depression [90]. The third trait, *impulsivity*, indicates difficulties in regulating behavioral responses [91]. The fourth trait, *sensation seeking* is characterized by the desire for intense and novel experiences [92].
- ***Responsibility.*** The Responsibility Attitudes Scale (RAS) [53] is a 26-item instrument used to assess subjective beliefs related to an inflated sense of responsibility (e.g., "I often feel responsible for things that go

wrong"). Responses are given on a 7-point Likert scale ranging from 1 (totally disagree) to 7 (totally agree). Japanese version of RAS was translated into Japanese by Ishikawa, Kobori, Ikota, and Shimizu (2014; see Chapter 2 for information on its development).

- ***Morality.*** The Contingencies of Self-Worth Scale [93] consists of 35 items divided into seven subscales, corresponding to seven domains on which people are likely to judge their self-worth. We used only the 5-item *virtue subscale* in order to assess participants' sense of worth related to virtue and morality. Sample items include "Whenever I follow my moral principles, my sense of self-respect gets a boost," and "I couldn't respect myself if I didn't live up to a moral code." Responses are given on a 7-point Likert scale ranging from 1 = "totally disagree" to 7 = "totally agree."

DESCRIPTIVE STATISTICS AND INTERNAL CONSISTENCY OF ASSESSMENTS

The means, standard deviations (SD), and internal consistency (Cronbach's α) of the measurements are presented in Table 5.

The results showed that the mean MPQ-Washing score was 6.98 (SD = 3.72) for females (n = 164) and 6.19 (SD = 3.63) for males (n = 72). The mean MPQ-Ideation score was 12.00 (SD = 5.49) for females and 11.68 (SD = 5.14) for males. There was no significant difference between female and male participants in MPQ-Ideation (t[234] = 1.01, p = .31) or MPQ-Washing scores (t[234] = 1.45, p = .15).

CORRELATIONS AMONG VARIABLES

Inter-correlations between the MPQ-J, BAI, BDI-II, OCI-Washing, personality traits (anxiety sensitivity, hopelessness, sensation seeking, and impulsivity), and cognitions (RAS and virtue) are presented in Table 6. Consistent with our predictions, MPQ-Washing was significantly correlated with MPQ-Ideation, BAI, BDI, OCI-Washing, anxiety sensitivity, sensation-seeking, impulsivity, RAS, and virtue scores. MPQ-Ideation was significantly correlated with BAI, BDI, OCI-Washing, anxiety sensitivity, hopelessness, impulsivity, RAS, and virtue scores.

Table 5. Means, standard deviations, and Cronbach's α coefficients of the measures

		Mean	SD	α
1	MPQ–Washing	6.74	3.70	.92
2	MPQ–Ideation	11.90	5.39	.80
3	BAI	14.55	11.53	.92
4	BDI	12.03	8.40	.88
5	OCI–Washing	4.59	3.22	.85
6	Anxiety sensitivity	11.69	2.90	.68
7	Hopelessness	16.40	3.77	.50
8	Sensation-seeking	12.98	3.85	.70
9	Impulsiveness	11.58	2.36	.78
10	RAS	100.28	24.14	.93
11	Virtue	21.79	4.98	.75

Note. MPQ–Washing = Subscale of the MPQ for hand washing; MPQ–Ideation = Subscale of MPQ for thoughts of pollution; BDI = Beck Depression Inventory version 2; BAI = Beck Anxiety Inventory; OCI–Washing = Washing subscale of the Obsessive Compulsive Inventory.

Table 6. Correlations for each variable

		MPQ–Washing	MPQ–Ideation
1	MPQ–Ideation	.45***	
2	BAI	.31***	.47***
3	BDI	.16*	.44***
4	OCI–Washing	.53***	.21**
5	Anxiety sensitivity	.35***	.32***
6	Hopelessness	-.02	.17*
7	Sensation-seeking	.15*	.06
8	Impulsivity	.14*	.13*
9	RAS	.46***	.47***
10	Virtue	.41***	.30***

Note. The first five instruments were used to confirm the psychometric properties of the MPQ–J and the remainder were used for hierarchical regression analysis.

MPQ–Ideation = Subscale of the MPQ–J thoughts of pollution; MPQ–Washing = Hand washing subscale of MPQ–J; BDI = Beck Depression Inventory version 2; BAI = Beck Anxiety Inventory; OCI–Washing = Washing subscale of the Obsessive Compulsive Inventory. $p < .05.$ ** $p < .01.$ *** $p < .001.$

DISCUSSION

In sum, factor analyses and an investigation of the test-retest reliability were conducted in Study 1. In that study, we demonstrated that the factor structure of the MPQ-J matched the two-factor model found by Cougle et al. [81]. In terms of test-retest reliability, the MPQ-J subscale scores at the two time points were moderately and significantly correlated, confirming the reliability of the MPQ-J. In Study 2, correlation analyses showed that both subscales of the MPQ-J were correlated with OCD symptoms (i.e., fear of contact contamination), depression symptoms, and cognitions associated with OCD (i.e., inflated sense of responsibility). This result is consistent with those of the original MPQ study, which showed that MPQ scores were significantly associated with the fear of contact contamination, depression, and inflated responsibility cognitions [81]. These results confirm the psychometric properties of the MPQ-J. In conclusion, the MPQ-J was found to be psychometrically robust, making it an appropriate tool to assess the symptoms of mental contamination in a Japanese population. The MPQ-J is the first psychometric measurement tool available to assess the symptoms of mental contamination in Asian cultures. Therapists treating Japanese patients with OCD or survivors of sexual assault may wish to use the MPQ-J as part of an assessment battery in order to identify clients at risk for mental contamination, thereby enabling therapists to offer more tailored and effective treatment.

CONCLUSION

VOCI-MC and MPQ measures the severity of mental contamination. Our research team conducted two studies to develop a Japanese version of the MPQ (MPQ-J). The studies confirmed the psychometric properties of the MPQ-J. The MPQ-J is the first psychometric measurement tool available to assess the symptoms of mental contamination in Asian cultures.

Chapter 6

COGNITIVE VULNERABILITY OF MENTAL CONTAMINATION

ABSTRACT

Cognitive models of anxiety disorders emphasize the key role of cognitive appraisals in increasing OC symptoms. Our research team tested the hypothesis that cognitive appraisals of an unwanted sexual experience predict indices of mental contamination (i.e. feeling of dirtiness, urge to wash, internal negative emotions, and external negative emotions). 148 female participants were asked to recall their most distressing unwanted sexual experiences. Indices of mental contamination and cognitive appraisals of the experience were then assessed. Hierarchical regression analyses demonstrated that a cognitive appraisal of perceived violation predicted all of the indices of mental contamination after controlling anxiety, depression, and fear of contact contamination.

INTRODUCTION

Cognitive theory of anxiety disorders emphasizes the key role of cognitive appraisals in increasing the subjective sense of anxiety, which in turn motivates safety-seeking behaviors [44-49]. For example, Salkovskis [49] proposed that an inflated sense of responsibility for harm to oneself or others (e.g., "I often feel responsible for things that go wrong.") are connected to intrusive thoughts (including images and/or impulses) and compulsions. In addition, cognitive appraisals focusing on the fear of physical harm (e.g., "I fear that I will get seriously ill,"), the fear of mental harm (e.g., "I fear that I will lose control of my mind."), or the fear of social harm (e.g., "I fear that I will be rejected by other people.") can result in the fear of contamination and the urge to wash [46-47].

This chapter demonstrates about cognitive vulnerability to mental contamination.

COGNITIVE VULNERABILITY TO MENTAL CONTAMINATION

Steil, Jung, and Stangier [76] suggested the concept of the "feeling of being contaminated," which differs from the concept of mental contamination. The mental contamination identified by Rachman [56] was explored in individuals who suffered from a feeling of dirtiness with an urge to wash and excessive washing behavior. However, "feeling of being contaminated" is possible to feel contaminated without an urge to wash or excessive washing behavior. Furthermore, they suggested using a more open, explorative, and focused definition of the feeling of being contaminated after childhood sexual abuse [76]. Based on this suggestion, they demonstrated that the development and maintenance of the feeling of being contaminated can be explained by two different routes, such as (a) negative appraisals after traumatization and (b) disgust towards perpetrator's body fluids/odors during traumatization [76].

(a) *Negative appraisals after traumatization.* Negative self-appraisals after the experience of sexual abuse induce the negative effects of self-disgust, shame, and self-contempt, thus leading to and preserving the sense of being contaminated. In this case, the feeling of being contaminated can be explained as a secondary trauma-related symptom that is based on negative cognitive appraisals and persistent negative images.

(b) *Disgust towards perpetrator's body fluids/odors during traumatization.* Some patients have complained that they already felt disgusted by the perpetrator's body fluids during the traumatic event and that the feeling of being contaminated appeared immediately afterwards. Consistent with Mowrer's two-factor learning theory [77], the feeling of contamination can also be explained by classical conditioning and the subsequent negative reinforcement of avoidance and escape. Thus, patients' reports of re-experienced touches or odors might be explained as sensory intrusions based on classical conditioning [68].

Cougle et al. [81] found that mental contamination, as measured by the MPQ, was associated with an inflated sense of responsibility [53], thought-action fusion (TAF) [82], and the symptoms of depression and OCD. Individuals with an inflated sense of responsibility feel the need to have absolute control over their mental lives, and are therefore prone to experiencing feelings of mental contamination after having an unwanted repugnant thought for which they feel responsible [81]. TAF refers to a set of cognitive biases involving faulty causal relationships between one's own thoughts and external reality [82]. These symptoms are related to the MPQ because mental contamination and TAF tend to co-occur among individuals who attach too much importance to their thoughts [81].

Rachman [47] suggested that the cognitions associated with external provocations of mental contamination resemble some of the cognitions associated with PTSD, as proposed by Ehlers and Clark [12]. For example, appraisals concerning one's responsibility for the traumatic event (e.g., "It was my fault") and others' violations of personal rules (e.g., "Others have not treated me fairly") would lead to PTSD and mental contamination. The experimental study conducted by Radomsky and Elliott [94] supports Rachman's cognitive theory of mental contamination. In that study, Radomsky and Elliott [94] asked participants to imagine a non-consensual kiss at a party as it was described on an audiotape, in order to provoke mental contamination. The researchers then measured participants' degree of mental contamination and their cognitive appraisals of the situation, such as a) their personal responsibility for the occurrence, b) the immorality of the offender's character, and c) the perceived violation. In a series of hierarchical regression analyses, three appraisal variables emerged as unique predictors of feelings of mental contamination aside from fear of contact contamination and specific and general sensitivities. However, while this study asked female participants to imagine a non-consensual kiss that was described on an audiotape, mental contamination can be evoked using other techniques. As previously discussed (see, Chapter 4), the *deliberate recall* of unwanted sexual experiences also evokes symptoms of mental contamination [55].

COGNITIVE APPRAISALS THAT EVOKE MENTAL CONTAMINATION

Our research team also tested the hypothesis that various cognitive appraisals (personal responsibility, immorality of the offender's character, and perceived violation) of an unwanted sexual experience differentially predict mental contamination in a Japanese sample [62]. For this purpose, female participants were asked to *deliberate recall* their most distressing unwanted sexual experiences.

METHOD

In this study, prospective participants were asked to contact the researchers to request a questionnaire. A total of 257 Japanese female undergraduates (age range: 18–28 years; $M = 18.45$, $SD = 1.51$) were enrolled as prospective participants in this study. Among them, 148 who had experienced one or more unwanted sexual experiences completed the full questionnaire. The procedure was as follows.

1. All participants completed the Japanese version of the SURPS-J [88] and the washing subscale of the OCI-J [43] to assess two personality traits (i.e., anxiety sensitivity and hopelessness) and degrees of contact contamination fear, respectively.

2. Participants were asked to complete the MCR upon entry into the study (pre-recall MCR). For more detail on the MCR, please see Chapter 4.

3. In order to induce mental contamination, participants who had had one or more unwanted sexual experiences were asked to remember what had happened, and to describe only their most distressing experience (no additional unwanted sexual experiences) on the questionnaire, in 100 words or less.

4. After participants had recalled and described their most distressing unwanted sexual experiences, they took the MCR again (post-recall MCR). Three appraisal variables were also assessed in the MCR by asking participants to rate their feelings of (a) responsibility for the unwanted sexual experience ("How responsible did you feel for the events?"); (b) the perceived violation ("How violated did you feel by

this offender's behavior?"); and (c) the immorality of the offender's character ("How morally wrong would you rate the offender's character?"). Each of these three questions was assessed via one item. Items were answered using a 0 to 100 SUDs scale, for which 0 represented "not at all" and 100 represented "completely."

RESULT

Using these data, we examined whether the three different types of cognitive appraisals would show incremental validity and explain further variance in the indices of mental contamination (after controlling for obsessive washing due to the fear of contact contamination and anxious and depressive personality traits). For this purpose, we conducted four hierarchical regression analyses using data from 148 participants. In each hierarchical regression analysis, variables in Model 1 included scores on OCI-Washing, age, and pre-recall scores as the independent variables. The variables entered in Model 2 were anxiety sensitivity and hopelessness. Model 3 included perceptions of personal responsibility for the unwanted sexual experience, the perceived violation, and the immorality of the offender's character.

In terms of feelings of dirtiness, a hierarchical regression analysis revealed that pre-recall scores for OCI-Washing ($\beta = .33, p < .01$) and dirtiness ($\beta = .23, p < .05$) significantly predicted post-recall feelings of dirtiness in Model 1 ($R^2 = .21, \Delta R^2 = .21, \Delta F[3, 144] = 12.03, p < .001$), but age did not (see Table 9). Anxiety sensitivity and hopelessness did not account for any unique variance in Model 2 ($R^2 = .26, \Delta R^2 = .05, \Delta F[3, 140] = 2.70, p < .10$). In Model 3, cognitive appraisals of responsibility ($\beta = .22, p < .05$), and perceived violation ($\beta = .36, p < .05$) accounted for unique variance in feelings of dirtiness, but the appraisal of the immorality of the offender's character did not ($R^2 = .41, \Delta R^2 = .15, \Delta F[3, 137] = 15.55, p < .001$) (Table 7).

In terms of the urge to wash, a hierarchical regression analysis revealed that the pre-recall urge to wash ($\beta = .23, p < .01$) predicted the post-recall urge to wash in Model 1 ($R^2 = .34, \Delta R^2 = .34, \Delta F[3, 144] = 24.46, p < .001$), but age and OCI-Washing scores did not (Table 7). Anxiety sensitivity and hopelessness did not account for any unique variance in Model 2 ($R^2 = .41, \Delta R^2 = .07, \Delta F[4, 140] = 3.52, p < .05$). The cognitive appraisal of the perceived violation ($\beta = .21, p < .05$) did account for unique variance in the post-recall urge to wash, but in Model 3, appraisals of responsibility for the unwanted sexual experience and the immorality of the offender's character did not ($R^2 = .47$, $\Delta R^2 = .06$, $\Delta F[3, 137] = 3.70$, $p < .05$) (Table 7).

Regarding INEs, a hierarchical regression analysis revealed that pre-recall INEs ($\beta = .50$, $p < .001$) predicted post-recall INEs in Model 1 ($R^2 = .29$, $\Delta R^2 = .29$, $\Delta F[3, 144] = 18.93$, $p < .001$), but age and OCI-washing scores did not (see Table 9). Anxiety sensitivity and hopelessness did not account for any unique variance in Model 2 ($R^2 = .33$, $\Delta R^2 = .04$, $\Delta F[4, 140] = 2.16$, $p < .10$). In Model 3, the appraisal of the perceived violation ($\beta = .41$, $p < .001$) accounted for unique variance in post-recall INEs, but appraisals of responsibility for the unwanted sexual experience and the immorality of the offender's character did not ($R^2 = .52$, $\Delta R^2 = .19$, $\Delta F[3, 137] = 16.84$, $p < .001$) (Table 8).

Finally, a hierarchical regression analysis for ENEs revealed that pre-recall ENEs ($\beta = .37$, $p < .001$) and OCI-Washing scores ($\beta = .18$, $p < .05$) predicted post-recall ENEs in Model 1 ($R^2 = .21$, $\Delta R^2 = .21$, $\Delta F[3, 144] = 11.98$, $p < .001$), but age did not. Anxiety sensitivity and hopelessness did not account for unique variance in Model 2 ($R^2 = .23$, $\Delta R^2 = .02$, $\Delta F[4, 140] = 1.19$, n.s.). In Model 3, the appraisal of the perceived violation ($\beta = .41$, $p < .001$) and immorality ($\beta = .16$, $p < .05$) accounted for unique variance in post-recall ENEs, but the appraisal of responsibility did not ($R^2 = .41$, $\Delta R^2 = .18$, $\Delta F[3, 137] = 17.06$, $p < .001$) (Table 8).

Table 7. Hierarchical regression analysis for dirtiness, and urge to wash

	Dirtiness			Urge to wash		
	R^2	ΔR^2	B	R^2	ΔR^2	B
Step 1						
Age	.21		.01	.34		.01
OCI-washing			.33**			.04
Pre-score			.23*			.23**
Step 2						
AS	.26	.05	.08	.41	.07*	.02
Hopeless			−.09			−.09
Step 3						
Responsibility	.41	.15***	.22*	.47	.06*	.04
Violation			.36**			.21*
Immorality			.10			.09

*$p < .05$. **$p < .01$. ***$p < .001$.

Table 8. Hierarchical regression analysis for INE, and urge to ENE

		INE			ENE		
		R^2	ΔR^2	B	R^2	ΔR^2	B
Step 1							
	Age	.29		.01	.21		.01
	OCI-washing			.10			.18*
	Pre-score			.50***			.37***
Step 2							
	AS	.33	.04*	.11	.23	.02	.06
	Hopeless			.05			−.05
Step 3							
	Responsibility	.52	.19***	.10	.41	.18***	.12
	Violation			.41***			.41***
	Immorality			.09			.16*

*$p < .05$. **$p < .01$. ***$p < .001$.

DISCUSSION

In sum, these hierarchical regression analyses showed that cognitive appraisals predicted mental contamination after controlling for the severity of contact contamination and personality traits. The study used a different procedure than that used by Radomsky and Elliott [94] to test the relationships between mental contamination and cognitive appraisals. As previously discussed, Radomsky and Elliott [94] used experimentally controlled stimuli to induce mental contamination for non-clinical participants, asking the participants to imagine a non-consensual kiss as described on an audiotape. This procedure made for high internal validity, permitting the researchers to control for extraneous variables. In contrast, the procedure used in this study —asking female participants to remember their most distressing unwanted sexual experiences—had high ecological validity [95]. Thus, by asking female participants to recall their most distressing unwanted sexual experiences, this study substantiates the hypothesis proposed by Radomsky and Elliott [94].

In hierarchical regression analyses, the cognitive appraisal of the perceived violation predicted all indices of mental contamination, after controlling for the severity of contact contamination and personality traits. This result supports the recent theoretical work that the cognitions associated with external provocations of mental contamination resemble some of the cognitions associated with PTSD [46-47].

Furthermore, in our study, the appraisal of the perceived violation was not the only predictor of mental contamination; appraisals of responsibility for the unwanted sexual experience predicted feelings of dirtiness, while appraisals of the immorality of the offender's character predicted ENEs (e.g., distress and anger). As mentioned previously, the findings of our study provide preliminary support for Radomsky and Elliott's [94] hypothesis that appraisals of responsibility and immorality predict mental contamination, using a different procedure. We also found that appraisals of personal responsibility for past trauma (e.g., "It was my fault that the incident happened") specifically predicted feelings of dirtiness as a form of mental contamination. This appraisal leads to guilt, along with PTSD symptoms [12]. As such, an exaggerated sense of responsibility may exacerbate mental contamination.

CONCLUSION

Our research team tested the hypothesis that cognitive appraisals of an unwanted sexual experience predict indices of mental contamination. Hierarchical regression analyses demonstrated that a cognitive appraisal of perceived violation predicted all of the indices of mental contamination after controlling anxiety, depression, and fear of contact contamination. The findings of our study provide preliminary support for the hypothesis that appraisals of an unwanted sexual experience predict mental contamination,

Chapter 7

ROLE OF WASHING BEHAVIOR IN MENTAL CONTAMINATION

ABSTRACT

Imagining a non-consensual kiss from an immoral man (Dirty Kiss task) can evoke feelings of mental contamination in non-clinical female participants. Fairbrother and Rachman [55] suggested that an ordinary sense of dirtiness (i.e., contact contamination) is immediately reduced by washing behaviours, whereas, feelings of mental contamination would not respond to washing. Our study investigated whether feelings of mental contamination are reduced by washing behavior or by simply waiting without washing. Female participants were split into two groups: washing (n=24; asked to wash their hands and mouth after the Dirty Kiss task) and non-washing (n=24; asked to wait without engaging in any behaviour after the Dirty Kiss task). Indices of mental contamination were administered before, immediately after, 5min after, and 20 min after the task. As a result of analysis, mental contamination scores did not significantly differ between the groups at any point. Our result demonstrated that mental contamination can be reduced by washing behaviour, although no more effective than waiting without washing.

INTRODUCTION

Rachman and Hodgson [35] suggested that compulsions such as washing reinforce OCD symptoms since the behavior seems to work by reducing negative emotions in the short term. Salkovskis [49] established that compulsions that serve to neutralize discomfort prevent patients with OCD from understanding that their fear will not actually come to pass (e.g., "I did not get sick because I washed my hands repeatedly"). Thus, the cognitive-behavioral theory of OCD suggests that neutralizing behaviors, such as washing, that are intended to reduce the fear of contamination do not actually reduce this fear in the long term; indeed, neutralizing behaviors may increase the urge to perform the compulsion, resulting in a vicious circle whereby obsessive-compulsive symptoms remain and even increase in severity [35] [49]. If feelings of mental contamination are also neutralized in the short-term by the washing behavior, the cognitive-behavioral theory of OCD suggested by Rachman and Hodgson [35] and Salkovskis [49] applies.

In addition, feelings of dirtiness in mental contamination may be subject to spontaneous decay if the affected person refrains from the neutralizing behavior, as earlier studies found with contact contamination (i.e. ordinal sense of contamination) [96] [97]. This notion provides the experimental underpinning for the exposure and response prevention (ERP) treatment of OCD. In this treatment, the patient's urge to engage in compulsive behavior (e.g., hand washing) is provoked by exposure to triggering stimuli (e.g., contact with a "contaminating" object) followed by a period in which the patient is prevented from yielding to this urge.

ROLE OF WASHING BEHAVIOR IN MENTAL CONTAMINATION

Our study [98] investigated whether feelings of mental contamination are reduced by washing behavior or by simply waiting without washing. If the indices of mental contamination are reduced to a greater degree by washing than by simply waiting without washing, the mental contamination levels of participants in a washing condition (individuals asked to engage in washing behavior) will be lower than will those among participants in a non-washing condition (individuals prevented from engaging in washing behavior). In addition, we investigated whether the subjective feeling of mental contamination spontaneously decay if the person experiencing the contamination does not engage in washing behavior. If washing behavior is unnecessary to reduce mental contamination, the non-washing group would be expected show significant declines in mental contamination levels over time.

METHOD

Forty-eight female undergraduates (age range: 18–25 years; M = 18.36, SD = 2.31) enrolled in psychology classes at a Japanese university participated in this experiment. To be included in the study, potential participants had to confirm in writing that they had never been diagnosed with a mental disorder. Prospective participants were asked to contact the researchers to schedule participation in the experiment.

ASSESSMENTS

The Mental Contamination Report (MCR; [36] [62] uses SUDs to assess feelings of dirtiness, the urge to wash, internal negative emotions (INEs), and external negative emotions (ENEs). In addition to indices of mental contamination, the MCR assesses how easily participants can imagine the scenario (one item). The possible score of each item ranges from 0 to 100. The Japanese version of this scale has adequate internal reliability and convergent validity [62]. We also administered the BDI-II, the BAI, and the OCI to measure participants' depression, anxiety, and obsessive-compulsive symptoms, respectively, to confirm that the sample consisted of non-clinical participants.

PROCEDURE

Participants were tested individually in the laboratory. The experimenter asked all participants to refrain from the following actions: writing memos or sentences, talking to the experimenter, using mobile phones, listening to music, and standing up from the chair. However, participants were told that they could stop the experiment at any time if they wished, simply by informing the experimenter. The procedure is described in Table 9.

Table 9. Procedure

No	Contents of the assessment and experimental tasks	
1	All participants were asked to complete the Beck Depression Inventory version 2 (BDI), Beck Anxiety Inventory (BAI), OCI–Washing (Washing subscale of the Obsessive Compulsive Inventory), and MCR (Pre).	
2	Then, all participants listened to an audio recording describing an non-consensual kiss from a man described as 'immoral'. The audio recording was the same as that used by Elliott and Radomsky [36]. All participants were asked to imagine that they were the woman described in the scenario, and that the events were happening to them at that moment (henceforth referred to as 'the Dirty Kiss task').	
3	The MCR was administered again (Dirty Kiss task).	
4	*Participants in the washing group:* They were asked to wash their hands using soap and their mouth using a bottle of water. They had 3 min to complete these washing behaviours but were free to do them in any manner they chose within this time limit. Since it took 2 min to give participants these instructions after the audio recording, the total time required to receive instructions and conduct in washing was 5 min.	*Participants in the non-washing group:* They were asked to simply wait in their seats without engaging in any other behaviour for 5 min. The experimenter asked all participants to refrain from the following actions: writing memos or sentences, talking to the experimenter, using mobile phones, listening to music, and standing up from the chair.
5	Indices of mental contamination were administered (MCR Post 1).	
6	All participants were then asked to wait in their seats without engaging in any other behaviour for 15 min.	
7	Indices of mental contamination were then assessed for the last time (MCR Post 2).	
8	Participants were then fully debriefed about the study and mental contamination, and were thanked for their participation.	

RESULTS

All participants were randomly assigned to either the washing group (n = 24; age range: 18–24 years; M = 18.42, SD = 2.23) or the non-washing group (n = 24; age range: 18–25 years; M = 18.23, SD = 2.61). The demographic and baseline characteristics and ease of imagining the audio scenario were compared for the two groups. There were no group differences in age ($t[46]$ = 1.36, p = .18) or the ease of imagining the scenario ($t[46]$ = 1.07, p = .26). There were also no group differences in BDI-II ($t[46]$ = .90, p = .25), BAI ($t[46]$ = 1.24, p = .13), or OCI washing scale ($t[46]$ = .97, p = .27) scores. The overall sample mean scores of the BDI-II, BAI, and OCI washing scale were 8.12 (SD = 7.42), 11.21 (SD = 10.20), and 4.25 (SD = 2.10), respectively, confirming the non-clinical nature of this sample.

Feelings of dirtiness as a form of mental contamination were based on responses to one item in the MCR. All the other subscale means were calculated using the summed scores of all items in each MCR subscale. In addition, we compared the groups in terms of pre-test scores on the indices of mental contamination (i.e., feelings of dirtiness, the urge to wash, INEs, and ENEs). The analyses showed that there were no group differences in feelings of dirtiness ($t[46]$ = 1.74, p = .08), the urge to wash ($t[46]$ = -1.86, p = .07), INEs ($t[46]$ = 0.39, p = .69), or ENEs ($t[46]$ = -1.25, p = .22). The results are presented in Table 10.

To evaluate the effects of washing behavior and waiting without washing on mental contamination, we used a 4 (time: Pre, Dirty Kiss task, Post 1, and Post 2) × 2 (Group: washing and non-washing) repeated measures MANOVA with feelings of dirtiness, the urge to wash, INEs, and ENEs as the four dependent variables. The analysis revealed a significant main effect of time ($F[12, 35]$ = 11.31, p < .001, η_p^2 = .743). However, there was no significant main effect of group ($F[4, 43]$ = 1.08, p = .09, η_p^2 = .109) or a group × time interaction ($F[12, 35]$ = 1.01, p = .13, η_p^2 = .101). Thus, there were no significant differences in the mental contamination levels between the washing and non-washing groups. The findings did not support the hypothesis that there are significant differences in the mental contamination levels between those who wash to neutralize their fears and those who do not.

Table 10. Means and standard deviations for MCR scores

Variables	Group	Pre	Immediately after Dirty Kiss task	Post 1	Post 2
Feeling of dirtiness	Experimental	23.89 (22.98)	56.67 (29.10)	31.50 (28.35)	27.17 (26.06)
	Control	16.09 (13.52)	66.09 (28.68)	38.04 (25.79)	35.00 (25.49)
Urge to wash	Experimental	10.29 (13.82)	46.46 (30.13)	19.47 (27.50)	15.37 (12.18)
	Control	18.26 (22.93)	52.50 (26.72)	25.69 (20.87)	21.70 (20.00)
INE	Experimental	7.83 (8.21)	37.28 (25.55)	15.03 (18.26)	13.16 (10.42)
	Control	8.88 (10.33)	45.25 (25.16)	21.82 (20.10)	19.42 (21.88)
ENE	Experimental	13.69 (3.56)	49.99 (5.09)	25.72 (4.48)	18.36 (3.40)
	Control	20.78 (3.47)	57.93 (4.97)	28.42 (4.38)	20.78 (3.32)

A one-way ANOVA was performed for each dependent variable in order to examine the results in more detail, using the Bonferroni correction for post-hoc comparisons. For feelings of dirtiness, the ANOVA revealed a significant main effect of time ($F[3, 138] = 37.09$, $p < .001$, $\eta_p^2 = .446$). Post-hoc analysis revealed significant differences in feelings of dirtiness between Pre and Dirty Kiss ($p < .001$), Pre and Post 1 ($p < .01$), Dirty Kiss and Post 1 ($p < .001$), and Dirty Kiss and Post 2 ($p < .001$) in the washing group. For the non-washing group, post-hoc analyses for time revealed significant differences in feelings of dirtiness between Pre and Dirty Kiss ($p < .001$), Pre and Post 1 ($p < .001$), Dirty Kiss and Post 1 ($p < .001$), Dirty Kiss and Post 2 ($p < .001$), and Post 1 and Post 2 ($p < .001$).

In the next set of analyses, an ANOVA with the urge to wash as the dependent variable revealed a significant main effect of time ($F[3, 138] = 37.80$, $p < .001$, $\eta_p^2 = .452$). Post-hoc analyses revealed significant differences in the urge to wash between Pre and Dirty Kiss ($p < .001$), Dirty Kiss and Post 1 ($p < .001$), and Dirty Kiss and Post 2 ($p < .001$) in both the washing and non-washing groups. In addition, only in the washing group, there was a significant difference between Pre and Post 1 ($p < .01$).

An ANOVA with INEs as the dependent variable revealed a significant main effect of time ($F[3, 138] = 32.10$, $p < .001$, $\eta_p^2 = .413$). Post-hoc analyses revealed significant differences in INEs between Pre and Dirty Kiss ($p < .001$), Pre and Post 1 ($p < .001$), Dirty Kiss and Post 2 ($p < .001$), and Post 1 and Post 2 ($p < .01$) in both groups.

Finally, an ANOVA with ENEs as the dependent variable revealed a significant main effect of time ($F[3, 138] = 37.18$, $p < .001$, $\eta_p^2 = .447$). Post-hoc analyses revealed significant differences in ENEs between Pre and Dirty Kiss ($p < .001$), Pre and Post 1 ($p < .001$), Dirty Kiss and Post 1 ($p < .001$), and Dirty Kiss and Post 2 ($p < .001$) in the washing group. For the non-washing group, post-hoc analyses revealed significant differences in ENEs between Pre and Dirty Kiss ($p < .001$), Pre and Post 1 ($p < .001$), Dirty Kiss and Post 1 ($p < .001$), Dirty Kiss and Post 2 ($p < .001$), and Post 1 and Post 2 ($p < .001$).

Thus, the findings support the hypothesis that the non-washing group would show significant declines in mental contamination levels over time. Furthermore, post-hoc analyses showed that scores on the feeling of dirtiness, the urge to wash, and ENEs measures taken immediately after the Dirty Kiss task were reduced at Post 1 (5 minutes). However, INEs scores declined only at Post 2 (20 minutes after the Dirty Kiss task).

DISCUSSION

In the present study, we investigated whether mental contamination provoked by imagining a non-consensual kiss is reduced by washing behavior or waiting without washing behavior. Since the Dirty Kiss task evoked indices of mental contamination for participants in the washing and non-washing groups, the manipulation was deemed effective. Japanese women may be especially reactive to feelings of mental contamination, as more than half of adult women have experienced one or more instances of sexual assault in their lifetimes [3] [62].

Our analyses indicated that the feeling of dirtiness, urge to wash, INEs, and ENEs did not significantly differ between the washing and non-washing groups. However, in both groups, analyses showed that scores on the feelings of dirtiness, urge to wash, and ENE measures taken immediately after the Dirty Kiss task had decreased by Post 1 (5min after the washing behaviour or waiting without washing). This result implies that mental contamination can be reduced by washing behaviour in a non-clinical sample, although it is no more effective than waiting without washing, at least for feelings of dirtiness, urge to wash, and ENEs. The result of our study would appear to support the cognitive-behavioral model, which implies that neutralizing behavior (e.g., washing) reinforces compulsions. People who engage in cleaning behavior may feel that it is effective in reducing the discomfort caused by mental contamination.

However, interestingly, scores on the INEs measure taken immediately after the Dirty Kiss task did not decline after the washing behavior. Thus, our study partly supports the theory proposed by Fairbrother and Rachman [47], which suggests that mental contamination is not particularly responsive to washing behaviors. Our study revealed an apparent difference between INEs (e.g., guilt and shame) and other aspects of mental contamination.

In the non-washing group, post-hoc analyses showed that scores on the feeling of dirtiness, the urge to wash, and ENE measures taken immediately after the Dirty Kiss task were reduced at Post 1 (5 minutes). These results suggest that much of the emotion associated with mental contamination declines within 5 minutes without engaging in neutralizing behavior. Thus, individuals without clinically relevant obsessive-compulsive symptoms can exhibit spontaneous decay [99] in mental contamination even without engaging in neutralizing behavior, such as washing. Furthermore, the spontaneous decay effect does not appear to be as quick for INEs (e.g., guilt or shame), as our results showed that INE scores did not decline at Post 1, but only at Post 2 (20 minutes after the Dirty Kiss task). The present study showed that because INEs take more time to spontaneously decay than do ENEs, distress caused by negative emotions about the self (e.g., guilt and shame) may be more prone to linger longer than negative emotions about the offender.

CONCLUSION

Our study was notable in its discovery that mental contamination in a non-clinical sample can be reduced by washing behavior, although washing is no more effective than waiting without washing, at least for feelings of dirtiness, the urge to wash, and ENEs. INEs, however, appear unresponsive to washing behavior. Furthermore, feelings of dirtiness, the urge to wash, and ENEs spontaneously decay within 5 minutes of being induced, whereas INEs appear to take 20 minutes to spontaneously decay.

Chapter 8

MENTAL CONTAMINATION AND LOW SELF-ESTEEM

ABSTRACT

There is a possibility that low self-esteem is a vulnerability factor for negative cognitions about the self, and that it predicts the feeling of mental contamination. Our research team tested the hypothesis that beliefs related to responsibility, morality, and self-esteem predict feelings of mental contamination as measured by the MPQ-J after controlling for contact contamination fears, the symptoms of depression and anxiety, and personality traits. Two hundred and thirty-six Japanese undergraduate students enrolled in Japanese universities participated in this study. All participants completed the questionnaire battery. Analysis showed that self-esteem made a negative contribution to MPQ-J. This result supports the hypothesis that low self-esteem often triggers negative cognitions about the self and constitutes a vulnerability factor for feelings of mental contamination.

INTRODUCTION

Mental contamination may be related not only to beliefs about responsibility and morality, but also to low self-esteem. Olatunji et al. [64] found that the feeling of mental contamination was fully mediated by trauma-related cognitions, such as negative cognitions about the self as assessed using the Posttraumatic Cognitions Inventory [100]. These cognitions would be likely evoked in individuals with low self-esteem and can be explained by negative core beliefs about the self [101]. Previous studies have indicated that individuals with low self-esteem are more vulnerable to post-traumatic symptoms and PTSD. Boscarino and Adams [102] investigated the predictors of PTSD after a disaster and found that decreased self-esteem was associated with PTSD. Among those who had suffered sexual assaults, a history of psychological abuse and violation has been shown to be uniquely associated with low self-esteem [103], while the effects of sexual victimization appears to lead to lower levels of self-esteem [104]. We hypothesized that low self-esteem is a predictor of mental contamination in individuals who have experienced sexual assault.

MENTAL CONTAMINATION AND LOW SELF-ESTEEM

Our research team tested the hypothesis that beliefs related to responsibility, morality, and self-esteem predict feelings of mental contamination as measured by the MPQ-J after controlling for contact contamination fears, the symptoms of depression and anxiety, and personality traits.

METHODS

Two hundred and thirty-six Japanese undergraduate students (68.64% female) enrolled in Japanese universities participated in this study (age range: 18–43; $M = 20.81$, $SD = 4.42$). All participants completed the questionnaire battery in approximately 30 minutes.

MEASURES

We administered the MPQ-J, RAS-J, BDI-II, BAI, OCI-Washing subscale, the Contingencies of Self Worth Scale (virtue scale), and the SURPS-J to all participants as part of the questionnaire battery (for more information on these scales, see pages Chapter 5). In addition, we administered the following scales, which have not been described in previous chapters.

Disgust Sensitivity

The Disgust Scale, Version 2, Short Form [105] consists of eight items selected using regression analysis from the original 32-item Disgust Scale, Version 2. We used this scale to assess disgust sensitivity, which is a basic negative emotion, the appraisal of which involves both a sense of offensiveness and revulsion accompanied by thoughts of contamination. The first four items of the measurement are assessed on a 4-point scale ranging from 1 (strongly disagree) to 4 (strongly agree) and include statements such as "I try to avoid letting any part of my body touch the toilet seat in a public restroom, even when it appears clean." The second four items are rated on a 4-point scale with differing anchors—from 1 (not disgusting at all) to 4 (very disgusting)—and include scenarios such as "You take a sip of soda and then realize that you picked up the wrong can, which a stranger had been drinking out of."

Self-Esteem

We used the Rosenberg Self-Esteem Scale (RSE; [107]) to measure self-esteem. The Japanese version of the scale (RSE-J) consists of ten items about self-esteem and was translated by Mimura and Griffiths [108]. Statements such as "I feel that I'm a person of worth, at least on an equal plane with others" are rated on a five-point Likert scale (1 = totally disagree to 5 = totally agree). The reliability and validity of the RSE-J were confirmed by Uchida and Ueno [109].

RESULTS

The correlations among the MPQ-J, BAI, BDI-II, OCI-Washing, personality traits (anxiety sensitivity, hopelessness, sensation seeking, impulsivity, and disgust sensitivity), and cognitions (RAS, virtue, and RSE–J) are presented in Table 11. Consistent with our predictions, MPQ-Ideation was significantly correlated with MPQ-Washing, BAI, BDI, OCI-Washing, anxiety sensitivity, RAS, and virtue scores. In addition, MPQ-Ideation was negatively correlated with RSE-J scores.

MPQ-Washing was significantly correlated with BAI, BDI, OCI-Washing, RAS, anxiety sensitivity, sensation-seeking, impulsivity, disgust sensitivity, RAS, and virtue. MPQ-washing was negatively correlated with RSE-J scores.

Table 11. Correlations for each variable

		MPQ-Ideation	MPQ-Washing
1	MPQ–Ideation	.45***	-
2	BAI	.47***	.31***
3	BDI	.44***	.16*
4	OCI–Washing	.21**	.53***
5	Anxiety sensitivity	.32***	.35***
6	Hopelessness	.17	-.02
7	Sensation–seeking	.06	.15*
8	Impulsivity	.13	.14*
9	Disgust	.08	.23**
10	Responsibility attitude scale	.47***	46***
11	Virtue	.30***	.41***
12	RSE–J	−.34***	−.39***

Note. MPQ–J = Japanese version of the Mental Pollution Questionnaire; MPQ–Ideation = Subscale of MPQ–J; MPQ–Washing = Subscale of MPQ–J; BDI = Beck Depression Inventory version 2; BAI = Beck Anxiety Inventory; OCI–Washing = Washing subscale of Obsessive Compulsive Inventory. * $p < .05$. ** $p < .01$. *** $p < .01$.

Then, we examined whether cognitions would show incremental validity and explain variance in the subscales of the MPQ-J beyond that explained by contact contamination fear, depression, anxiety, and personality traits. For this, we conducted two hierarchical regression analyses. The first predicted MPQ-Ideation, and the second, MPQ-Washing. Each regression analysis comprised three steps. In step 1, age, gender (female = 0, male = 1), OCI-Washing, BDI-II, and BAI were entered as predictors. In step 2, personality traits (anxiety sensitivity, hopelessness, sensation seeking, impulsivity, and disgust sensitivity) were entered. Finally, cognitions (RAS, virtue, and RSE-J) were entered in step 3. These results are presented in Table 12.

Table 12. Hierarchical regression analyses

	MPQ–Ideation			MPQ–Washing		
	R^2	ΔR^2	B	R^2	ΔR^2	β
Step 1—Symptom						
Age	.29		.01	.28		.01
Gender			.01			−.11
OCI–Washing			.04			.38**
BDI			.12			−.07
BAI			.30**			.09
Step 2—Personality						
AS	.31	.02	.02	.33	.05**	.16*
Hopelessness			−.09			−.05
SS			−.07			−.06
Impulsivity			−.03			−.02
Disgust			−.03			−.04
Step 3—Cognition						
RAS	.38	.07**	.24**	.40	.07**	.15*
Virtue			.10			.19**
RSE–J			−.16*			−.18**

Note. MPQ–J = Japanese version of the Mental Pollution Questionnaire; MPQ–Ideation = Subscale of MPQ–J; MPQ–Washing = Subscale of MPQ–J; BDI = Beck Depression Inventory; BAI = Beck Anxiety Inventory; OCI–Washing = Washing subscale of Obsessive Compulsive Inventory; AS = Anxiety Sensitivity; SS = Sensation–Seeking; RAS = Responsibility Attitude Scale; RSE–J = Rosenberg Self–Esteem scale.
* $p < .05$. ** $p < .01$.

The results of the hierarchical regression analysis for MPQ-Ideation revealed that, only BAI (β = .30, $p < .01$) predicted MPQ–ideation in step 1, and personality trait variables did not show a significant regression coefficient in step 2. RAS (β = .24, $p < .01$) made a unique contribution to MPQ–ideation, and RSE–J (β = −.16, $p < .05$) a negative contribution, but virtue did not make a contribution to MPQ–ideation in step 3. Regarding MPQ–washing, OCI–washing scores (β = .38, p < .01) predicted MPQ–washing in step 1, and anxiety sensitivity (β = .16, p < .05) showed a significant regression coefficient in step 2, while other personality scales did not. In step 3, RAS (β = .15, $p < .05$) and virtue (β = .19, $p < .01$) made unique contributions to MPQ–washing, and RSE–J (β = −.18, $p < .01$) made a negative contribution to MPQ–washing.

DISCUSSION

The main purpose of this study was to investigate the cognitions that constitute vulnerability factors for the feelings of mental contamination as measured by the MPQ-J. Regarding inflated responsibility, consistent with our predictions, RAS made a unique contribution to the MPQ-J subscales above and beyond that provided by contact contamination fears, the symptoms of depression and anxiety, and personality traits. Individuals with a high sense of responsibility felt more responsible for negative occurrences (e.g., "I often feel responsible for things that go wrong."), and this cognitive appraisal appears to trigger the feeling of mental contamination. For example, when one experiences a feeling of responsibility or shame for participating in a situation deemed immoral, one will be more likely to experience these internal, emotionally charged feelings of dirtiness [47].

In terms of cognitions in the importance of a high moral standard, hierarchical regression analyses showed that the virtue scale made a unique contribution to the MPQ-J total score and to MPQ-Washing beyond that provided by contact contamination fears, the symptoms of depression and anxiety, and personality traits. Individuals with strong moral cognitions see offenders as immoral when they encounter or remember negative events. This appraisal seems to trigger feelings of mental contamination, particularly the urge to wash. According to Rachman [47], cognitions associated with mental contamination include moral precepts. However, inconsistent with our prediction, the virtue scales did not make a unique contribution to MPQ-Ideation. This study suggests that beliefs about high moral standards may predict the urge to wash in order to relieve distress, rather than predicting a sense of inward contamination.

Self-esteem made a negative contribution to MPQ-Ideation and MPQ-Washing. This result supports the hypothesis that low self-esteem often triggers negative cognitions about the self and constitutes a vulnerability factor for feelings of mental contamination. For example, individuals with borderline personality disorder (BPD) who have unstable self-esteem [110] may be at greater risk of feelings of mental contamination. Baer et al. [111] showed that approximately 25% of inpatients with BPD had OCD symptoms, although their OCD was not confined to mental contamination fears. Furthermore, low self-esteem seems to be related to the vulnerability to perceived violation, which Ehlers and Clark [12] described as being associated with cognitions regarding unfairness (e.g., "Others have not treated me fairly"). Perceived violation has been found to be a predictor of mental contamination [94].

Kuppens, Van Mechelen, Smits, De Boeck, and Ceulemans [112] investigated the relationship between low self-esteem and situations that involve violation. They found that participants with low self-esteem ascribed greater unfairness to and expressed more negative emotions toward the person who violated them than did participants with high self-esteem. Furthermore, individuals with low self-esteem are likely to think that they were treated more disrespectfully and unfairly, and then conclude that they have been violated when they meet the violator or remember the negative events. These thoughts may trigger feelings of mental contamination. There is a possibility that low esteem predicts feelings of mental contamination via vulnerability to perceived violation. This perspective could be beneficial in targeting interventions for patients with low self-esteem [113] [114]. In conclusion, these results have shown that individuals with a high sense of responsibility, strong moral standards, and low self-esteem seem to develop more severe mental contamination.

CONCLUSION

Our research team hypothesized that mental contamination may be related not only to cognitions about responsibility and morality, but also to low self-esteem. Analysis showed that self-esteem made a negative contribution to MPQ-J. This result supports the hypothesis that low self-esteem often triggers negative cognitions about the self and constitutes a vulnerability factor for feelings of mental contamination.

Chapter 9

CLINICAL IMPLICATIONS

ABSTRACT

Cognitive-behavioral therapy appears to be beneficial in reducing or treating victims of sexual assault suffering from PTSD and mental contamination. For example, prolonged exposure therapy is a type of cognitive behavioral therapy aimed at helping survivors emotionally process their experiences. In addition, trauma-focused cognitive behavioral therapy is an evidence-based psychotherapy shown to aid traumatized children and adolescents as well as their caregivers. Rachman [47] suggested some key points to consider in using the cognitive-behavioral approach to treat mental contamination. In addition, some researchers have proposed that the treatment should focus on correcting cognitive processes, augmented by behavioral experiments, addressing self-esteem, Theory A and Theory B, and cognitive restructuring and imagery.

INTRODUCTION

The treatment protocol based on the cognitive-behavioral theory appears to be beneficial in reducing or treating victims of sexual assault suffering from PTSD and mental contamination. Prolonged exposure therapy and Trauma-focused CBT are examples. This chapter demonstrates some key points to consider in using the cognitive-behavioral approach to treat mental contamination.

PROLONGED EXPOSURE THERAPY FOR PTSD

Prolonged exposure (PE) therapy is a type of cognitive behavioral therapy (CBT) aimed at helping survivors emotionally process their experiences. Currently, this therapy is the gold standard psychotherapeutic approach to treating PTSD [132-136]. PE was derived from the long tradition of "exposure therapy," which is usually used to treat anxiety disorders. In PE, patients are helped to confront anxiety-arousing situations or stimuli in a safe environment in the hopes that the excessive fear and anxiety derived from these situations will decrease with repeated exposure. PE is rooted in the emotional processing theory of PTSD [138]. This theory emphasizes that a specific type of processing—that is, emotional processing—of the traumatic event must take place for PTSD symptoms to fade. According to emotional processing theory, fear is represented in memory as a "program" for escaping danger. The structure of a fear response—called a fear network—comprises different types of information, including that on the fearful situation, person, or phenomenon, called *feared stimuli* (e.g., "adult men"); the actual sensations of the fear response (e.g., "an increase in heart rate"); and the meaning the individual associates with the stimuli (e.g., "adult men are dangerous") and response (e.g., "a fast heartbeat means that I am afraid"). It is believed that fear networks are the mechanism governing the development of PTSD symptoms. Emotional processing theory suggests that repeated exposure to a feared stimulus can change how fear networks respond to that stimulus. For this to happen, the network must first be activated by a given feared stimulus, after which new information must be encoded that is incompatible with information already in the fear network. This is accomplished through *habituation*, that is, the experience of getting used to certain feelings or stimuli such that eventually they are perceived more as irritating than as truly dangerous. Repeatedly accessing a feared stimulus until the fear response attenuates allows for the encoding of new adaptive information incompatible with the feared stimulus (e.g., that it is not dangerous). Following this theory of emotional processing, a typical PE treatment program includes the following procedures:

1. Psychoeducation on normal reactions to trauma, wherein the therapist and patients discuss the common reactions to traumas.
2. Breathing retraining, wherein the therapist teaches patients how to breathe in a calming way in order to slow it down, decreasing the amount of oxygen in the blood and thus decreasing anxiety.

3. Repeated in vivo (i.e., in real life) exposure is practiced for situations, people, or activities that patients are avoiding.
4. Repeated, prolonged imagery-based exposure is practiced to alter trauma memories—namely, patients attempt to revise the trauma in their imaginations.

In OCD, repeated exposure to the target of an obsession or intrusive thought while refraining from engaging in a particular ritual or compulsion serves to disconfirm the individual's maladaptive beliefs about the importance of the ritual in preventing harm.

TRAUMA-FOCUSED CBT [116]

Trauma-focused CBT [115-116] is an evidence-based psychotherapy shown to aid traumatized children and adolescents as well as their caregivers. It is designed to improve emotional and behavioral problems in children and treat negative beliefs and attributions related to the abusive experiences. In addition, the treatment aims to provide support and skills to teach non-offending parents to cope effectively with their own emotional distress and optimally respond to their children.

The treatment focuses on reducing the conditioned emotional associations to memories and triggers of the trauma, maladaptive cognitions about the events, and negative attributions about the self, others, and the world. Non-offending parents are included in the treatment process to increase support for the child, reduce parental distress, and teach appropriate strategies for managing the child's maladaptive behavior. Family sessions that include siblings may also be conducted to enhance positive communication among family members. Trauma-focused CBT combines elements drawn from:

- Cognitive therapy, which aims to change behavior by addressing a person's thoughts or perceptions, particularly those thinking patterns that create distorted or unhelpful views.
- Behavioral therapy, which focuses on modifying habitual responses (e.g., anger, fear) to identified situations or stimuli.
- Family therapy, which examines patterns of interactions among family members to identify and alleviate problems.

Trauma-focused CBT has proven effective for children exposed to a variety of traumatic events and has received considerable empirical support from studies with abused children [116-124]. It has been used in individual, family, and group therapy and in office- and school-based settings.

Cognitive Behavioral Therapy for Mental Contamination

The treatment protocol based on the cognitive-behavioral theory of mental contamination [47] appears to be beneficial in reducing or treating patients suffering from mental contamination. Rachman [47] previously suggested that largely cognitive approaches are more suitable for treating mental contamination than are approaches rooted in correcting behaviors, such as exposure-based treatment. Researchers have proposed that the treatment should focus on correcting cognitive processes, augmented by behavioral experiments to test key cognitions, rather than on the traditional exposure work used in the treatment of an ordinary sense of dirtiness (i.e., contact contamination) [47] [62] [78] [94]. This intervention is based on obtaining a thorough understanding of the current problem and its impact on the patient. Patients are asked to recall a specific and recent example of mental contamination to elicit thoughts, feelings, and counterproductive behaviors (e.g., "What do you do to cope with your fears?"). Below are some key points to consider in using the cognitive-behavioral approach to treat mental contamination [47] [62] [78].

1. Gathering information about the sources of contamination, in particular human sources, and any hypervigilance to these sources. This step includes asking questions about vulnerability to morphing (taking on the undesirable characteristics of another person). The therapist might ask, "Are you worried you might become like them?" and "How would that happen?" The therapist should also ascertain whether the person believes that they are able to take on the positive characteristics of a desirable person ("Can you ever pick up positive characteristics?").

2. Taking a detailed history of the development of the mental contamination, including questions about when the problem started, the rate of onset, how the client makes sense of the problem, and personal vulnerability. This includes questions such as, "How do you make sense of the problem?" "If that happened to someone else, do

you think they would become contaminated?" "What was happening in your life when the problem first started?" and "What would be the worst outcome?"

3. A focus on previous or current physical and psychological violations and betrayals [79]. This typically began by asking clients, "Can you tell me about anyone who has been particularly helpful to you? What were their characteristics?" Then, the therapist goes on to ask questions such as, "Can you tell me about anyone who has been particularly unhelpful to you? You don't have to identify them if you don't wish to. What were their characteristics?"

4. Obtaining information about the way the mental contamination spreads. Patients are asked, "Do new items/people/places ever become contaminated? How do they become contaminated?"

5. A focus on mental imagery. Asking clients, "Are there any pictures that cause you to feel contaminated?" This also includes questions about protective images. "Are there any pictures in your mind that you use to protect yourself?" Some patients report protective imagery shields, which can be further explored with questions about the effort it takes to create the protective shield and its effectiveness.

A variety of cognitive interventions are used to modify maladaptive cognitions, such as changing cognitive appraisals and interpretations of the sources of contamination; modifying self-generated contamination by helping the patient recognize the effects of maladaptive misinterpretations of the significance of the feelings of contamination; and separating feelings of anger, aversion, and disgust from mental contamination. A preliminary case study has shown that these are effective techniques in reducing crippling levels of mental contamination fear [125]. Coughtrey et al. [78] reported on a case series of 12 participants with OCD. All participants experienced 10 to 20 sessions of CBT focusing on mental contamination. As a result of the CBT treatment, 7 participants no longer met the diagnostic criteria for OCD and mental contamination. In addition, these gains were maintained at a 6-month follow-up assessment. Their study had significant implications for clinical practice, guiding the treatment of OCD with mental contamination and suggesting that CBT is an effective treatment approach.

In the following sections, I explain how to treat patients with a fear of mental contamination using cognitive therapy based on the approach suggested by Coughtrey et al. [78].

Behavioral Experiments

Bennett–Levy [114] defined that "Behavioural experiments are planned experimential activities, based on experimentation or observation, which are undertaken by patients in or between cognitive therapy sessions". Behavioural experiments test the validity of the patients' existing beliefs about themselves, others, and world [114].

Behavioral experiments are particularly useful for exploring patients' TAF and morality, which are common problems associated with mental contamination. The fear of mental contamination is often maintained by such cognitions [81]. Behavioral experiments to change TAF and morality have included a modification of Rachman et al.'s experiment [78] [126], in which clients are asked to write down a sentence stating that they wish harm on a loved one in order to explore the influence of TAF. In addition to this, after completing a survey about appropriate moral standards, clients conduct an experiment in which they act "as if" they had the same moral standards as others for one day, and then on the next day they revert to their own (usually higher) moral standards. Feelings of contamination on the contrasting days are assessed and conclusions are drawn about the impact of high moral standards on their contamination fears [78].

Addressing Self-esteem

In CBT for mental contamination, it may be effective to change the meaning of the source of the contamination. In addition, some cognitive techniques to reinterpret the meaning of self-generated contamination and self-esteem may be important in order to address the feeling of mental contamination. Issues of self-identity are particularly relevant when tackling beliefs about morphing. Clients can complete behavioral experiments (i.e., making a list of personal characteristics that are stable and unchanging) to reinforce their self-identity and increase self-esteem, thereby reducing their vulnerability to morphing fears.

"Theory A and Theory B"

Salkovskis pointed out that "*The most effective way of changing a misinterpretation ... is to help the person come up with an alternative, less threatening interpretation of his or her experience* [127]." Cognitive methods include helping the client see an issue from another perspective, through discussion and cognitive restructuring. One such method is "Theory A and Theory B" [128], which involves reframing a problem as the result of a belief or worry, rather than as a result of an actual situation/fact. This also includes experiments in which the client and therapist compare two theories explaining the feeling of contamination. For example, they may deliberately try to spread the contamination to test whether the person is truly contaminated (Theory A) or whether it is a problem in their thinking (Theory B).

Imagery

In recent years, researchers have shown growing interest in the use of imagery in CBT. Imagery interventions in CBT are based on the premise that mental imagery has a powerful impact on emotion, and that mental imagery in a clinical setting can be a powerful psychotherapeutic tool for alleviating emotional distress [130].

A significant amount of treatment time is devoted to understanding the role of images in triggering and maintaining mental contamination [47] [78]. This is initially assessed using the following test. Clients are asked to rate their current feelings of contamination from 0 to 100, and are then asked to close their eyes and form a picture of their best friend and think about him/her as clearly as they can. They are asked to raise one of their hands when they have formed a vivid image in their mind and to keep thinking about this person. Clients then rerate their contamination levels. Clients are then asked to close their eyes again and to imagine the following: "you are walking down the street, you turn the corner and you see [source of contamination] or have a contaminating thought." After this imagery, clients are asked to rerate their feelings of contamination and describe how they are feeling. The therapist asks the following questions: "Where in your body do you feel the contamination? When you feel like this, what do you have the urge to do?" In a behavioral experiment assessing whether protective images actually prolong feelings of contamination in the long term, clients are encouraged to drop their protective images to examine the effect. They are encouraged to distance themselves from any images that cause feelings of contamination and rescript them [78] [129].

COGNITIVE RESTRUCTURING AND IMAGERY

Steil, Jung, and Stangier [76] also use cognitive restructuring and imagery modification to treat the distressing feeling of contamination among adult survivors of childhood sexual abuse. The therapist and patient assess the contents of the feeling of contamination. The therapist then teaches the patient to use the Internet to calculate the number of times the patient's dermal cells in trauma-related body regions have been completely replaced since the last contact with the perpetrator. Skin cells are replaced every four to six weeks, and the cells of mucous membranes are replaced even more often [131]. Therefore, if the last contact with the perpetrator happened 20 years ago, the patient will calculate that the dermal cells of her vagina/mouth/hands have been completely replaced at least 240 times since that time. Finally, the therapist and patient discuss what this new information means to the patient (i.e., "Not one of the dermal cells that cover my body and orifices now has been in contact with the perpetrator or his body fluids.").

The therapist then leads the patient through an imagery exercise in which they rescript the skin renewal. As described by Steil, Jung, and Stangier [76], one patient might imagine that she is wearing a diving suit, which she takes off; at the same time, she takes off her contaminated skin completely. Then, the therapist instructs the patient to activate the feeling of being contaminated and the related distressing images continually until the feeling reaches a moderate intensity. Afterwards, the patient is instructed to use his/her idiosyncratic imagery of his/her old skin being replaced with new skin. For homework, the patient is asked to listen to a tape of the guided imagery modification session at least once a day over a period of seven days.

To evaluate the feasibility and efficacy of cognitive restructuring and imagery modification, Steil, Jung, and Stangier [76] consecutively treated nine women suffering from chronic PTSD and feelings of mental contamination. Patients rated the intensity, vividness, and uncontrollability of their contamination feeling and its accompanying distress, and completed the Posttraumatic Diagnostic Scale (PDS). The results suggested that cognitive restructuring and imagery modification has the potential to reduce the feelings of contamination, as well as PTSD symptoms, after childhood sexual abuse.

CONCLUSION

CBT appears to be beneficial in reducing or treating victims of sexual assault suffering from PTSD and men2tal contamination. In addition, some cognitive intervention, such as behavioral experiments, addressing self-esteem, Theory A and Theory B, and cognitive restructuring and imagery, appears to be beneficial in reducing or treating patients suffering from mental contamination.

ACKNOWLEDGMENTS

The author would like to express my sincere gratitude to my supervisor, Professor Eiji Shimizu for providing me this precious study opportunity as a Ph. D. student in his laboratory. I also express the deepest gratitude to Ph.D. Osamu Kobori who contributed to the conceptualization and design of the study about mental contamination. I acknowledge the assistance and advice of many colleagues including H. Komuro, and D. Ikota who have been close colleagues. Another colleague at the Chiba City Mental Clinic who made helpful contributions is Dr. M. Igarashi.

Finally, I would also like to express my gratitude to my dear father, Mikio Ishikawa, dear my mother, Chikako Ishikawa, dear my brother, Yusuke Ishikawa and dear my fiancé, Asami Imasato for their endless love, understanding, support, encouragement and sacrifice throughout my study.

REFERENCES

[1] US Department of Health and Human Services, Office on Women's Health (2012). *Sexual assault fact sheet: what is sexual assault?* Retrieved from http://www.womenshealth.gov/publications/our-publications/ fact-sheet/sexual-assault.cfm.

[2] Konishi, T. (1996). A survey about sexual assault in Japanese students. *JASS Proceedings, 8*, 28-47.

[3] Sasagawa, M., Konishi, T., Ando, K., Sato, S., Takahashi, M., Ishi, T. and Sato, S. (1998). Sexual victimization in Japanese adult women. *The Japanese Association of Criminology, 64*, 202–212.

[4] Burgess, A. W. & Lynda, L. H. (1974). "Rape Trauma Syndrome". *American Journal of Psychiatry,* 131 (9) 981–986.

[5] American Psychiatric Association (2000). *Diagnostic and Statistical Manual of Mental Disorders (text rev.,4th ed.).* Arlington, VA: APA.

[6] McCann, I. L., & Pearlman, L. A. (1990). *Psychological trauma and the adult survivor: theory, therapy, and transformation.* New York: Brunner and Mazel.

[7] Roth, S., & Newman, E. (1991). The process of coping with sexual trauma. *Journal of Traumatic Stress, 4,* 279–297.

[8] Foa, E. B., & Riggs, D. S. (1993). Post-traumatic stress disorder in rape victims. In (pp. 272–303). J. Oldham, M. B. Riba, & A. Tasman, *Annual review of psychiatry*, (Vol. 12). Washington, DC: American Psychiatry Association.

[9] Brewin, C. R., Dalgleish, T., & Joseph, S. (1996). A dual representation theory of post-traumatic stress disorder. *Psychological Review*, 103, 670–686.

[10] Horowitz, M. J. (1997). Stress response syndromes. PTSD grief and adjustment disorders. Northvale, NJ: Jason Aronson.

[11] Foa, E. B., & Rothbaum, B. O. (1998). Treating the trauma of rape. Cognitive-behaviour therapy for PTSD. New York: Guilford.

[12] Ehlers, A. and Clark, D. M. (2000). A cognitive model of posttraumatic stress disorder. *Behaviour Research and Therapy, 38,* 319–345.

[13] Dunmore, E., Clark, D.M., & Ehlers, A. (2001). A prospective study of the role of cognitive factors in persistent posttraumatic stress disorder after physical or sexual assault. *Behaviour Research and Therapy*, 39, 1063-1084.

[14] Wegner, D. M. (1989). *White bears and other unwanted thoughts: suppression, obsession, and the psychology of mental control.* New York: Viking.

[15] Davis, M. I., & Clark, D. M. (1998). Thought suppression produces a rebound effect with analogue post-traumatic intrusions. *Behaviour Research and Therapy*, 36, 571–582.

[16] Shiperd, J. C., & Beck, J. G. (1999). The effects of suppressing trauma-related thoughts on women with rape-related posttraumatic stress disorder. *Behaviour Research and Therapy*, 37, 99–112.

[17] Foa, E. B., Molnar, C., & Cashman, L. (1995). Change in rape narratives during exposure therapy for post-traumatic stress disorder. Journal of Traumatic Stress, 8, 675–690.

[18] van der Kolk, B. A., & Fisler, R. (1995). Dissociation and the fragmentary nature of traumatic memories: overview and exploratory study. *Journal of Traumatic Stress*, 8, 505–525.

[19] Conway, M. A. (1997). *Introduction: what are memories?* In M. A. Conway, Recovered memories and false memories (pp. 1–22). Oxford: Oxford University Press.

[20] World Health Organization (1999). *The Newly Defined Burden of Mental Problems, Fact Sheet* (No. 217). Geneva: WHO.

[21] Kawakami, N. (2007). *Scientific Research from the Japanese Ministry of Health, Labor and Welfare, Study on epidemiology about mental health, Research report in 2007.* Tokyo: Ministry of Health, Labor and Welfare.

[22] Goodman, W., Price, L., Rasmussen, S. A., Mazure, C., Fleischmann, R. L., Hill, C. L., Heninger, G. R., Charney, D. S. (1989). The Yale-Brown Obsessive Compulsive Scale, I: development, use, and reliability. *Arch Gen Psychiatry*, 46:1006–1011.

References

85

[23] Matsunaga, H., Maebayashi, K., Hayashida, K., Okino, K., Matsui, T., Iketani, T., Kiriike, N., and Stein, D. J. (2008). Symptom structure in Japanese patients with obsessive-compulsive disorder. *American Journal of Psychiatry*, *165*, 251-253.

[24] Rasmussen, S. A. and Eisen, J. L. (1992). The epidemiology and clinical features of obsessive-compulsive disorder. *Psychiatric Clinics of North America*, *15*, 743–758.

[25] Nakajima, T., Nakamura, M., Taga, C., Yamagami, S., Kiriike, N., Nagata, T., Saitoh, M., Kinoshita, T., Okajima, Y., Hanada, M., et al. (1995). Reliability and validity of the Japanese version of the Yale-Brown Obsessive-Compulsive Scale. *Psychiatry and Clinical Neurosciences*, 49, 121–126.

[26] DeVeaugh-Geiss, J., Landau, P., and Katz, R. (1989). Treatment of OCD with clomipramine. *Psychiatric Annals*, 19, 97–101.

[27] Foa, E. B., Kozak, M. J., Salkovskis, P. M., Coles, M. E. and Amir, N. (1998). The validation of a new obsessive-compulsive disorder scale: the obsessive-compulsive inventory (OCI). *Psychological Assessment*, *10*, 206–214.

[28] Clark, D.A. (2004). *Cognitive-Behavioral Therapy for OCD*. New York: The Guilford Press; 2004.

[29] Baer, L. (1991). Getting control: overcoming obsessions and compulsions. Boston: Little Brown.

[30] Hamagaki, S., Takagi, S., Urushihara, Y., Ishisaka, Y., and Matumoto, M. (1990). Development and Use of the Japanese Version of the Self-Report Yale-Brown Obsessive Compulsive Scale. *Psychiatria et neurologia Japonica*, 101, 152-168.

[31] Wu, K. D., Watson, D., and Clark, L. A. (2007). A self-report version of the Yale-Brown obsessive-compulsive scale symptom checklist: psychometric properties of factor-based scales in three samples. *Journal of Anxiety Disorders*, 21, 644–661.

[32] Ólafsson, R.P., Snorrason, I., and Smári, J. (2010). Yale-Brown Obsessive Compulsive Scale: Psychometric Properties of the Self-Report Version in a Student Sample. *Journal of Psychopathology and Behavioral Assessment*, 32, 226–235.

[33] Hodgson, R. J., and Rachman, S. J. (1977). Obsessional-compulsive complaints. *Behaviour Research and Therapy*, 15, 389–395.

[34] Tadai, T., Nakamura, M., Okazaki, S., Nakajima, T. (1996). The prevalence of obsessive-compulsive disorder in Japan: a study of

students using the Maudsley Obsessional-Compulsive Inventory and DSM-III-R. *Psychiatry and Clinical Neurosciences*, 49, 39–41.

[35] Rachman, S., and Hodgson, R. (1980). *Obsessions and compulsions.* Englewood Cliffs, NJ: Prentice Hall.

[36] Elliott, C. M. and Radomsky, A. S. (2009). Analyses of mental contamination: Part I, experimental manipulations of morality. *Behaviour Research and Therapy, 47*, 995–1003.

[37] Taylor, S. (1995). Assessment of obsessions and compulsions: Reliability, validity, and sensitivity to treatment effects. *Clinical Psychology Review*, 15, 261–296.

[38] Sanavio, E. (1998). Obsessions and compulsions: The Padua Inventory. *Behaviour Research and Therapy*, 26, 169–177.

[39] Sugiura, Y., Tanno, Y. (2000). Self-report inventory of obsessive-compulsive symptoms: Reliability and validity of the Japanese version of Padua Inventory. *Archives of Psychiatric Diagnostics and Clinical Evaluation*, 11, 175–189.

[40] Freeston, M. H., Ladouceur, R., Rhe´aume, J., Letarte, H., Gagnon, F., and Thibodeau, N. (1994). Self-report of obsessions and worry. *Behaviour Research and Therapy*, 32, 29–36.

[41] Zhong, J., Wang, C., Liu, J., Qin, M., Tan, J., and Yi, C. (2011). Psychometric properties of the Padua Inventory in Chinese college samples. *Psychological Report*, 109, 803-818.

[42] Simonds, L.M., Thorpe, S.J., Elliot, S.A. (2000). The Obsessive Compulsive Inventory: psychometric properties in a non-clinical student sample. *Behavioural and Cognitive Psychotherapy*, 28, 153–159.

[43] Ishikawa, R., Kobori, O., and Shimizu, E. (2014) . Development and validation of the Japanese version of the Obsessive-Compulsive Inventory. BMC Research Notes, Doi: 10.1186/1756-0500-7-306.

[44] Rachman, S. (1997). A cognitive theory of obsessions. *Behaviour Research and Therapy*, 35, 793–802.

[45] Rachman, S. (1998). A cognitive theory of obsessions: elaborations. *Behaviour Research and Therapy*, 36, 385–401.

[46] Rachman, S. (2004). Fear of contamination. *Behaviour Research and Therapy*, 42, 1227–1255.

[47] Rachman, S. (2006). *The Fear of Contamination: assessment and treatment (Cognitive behaviour therapy: Science and practice)*. Oxford: Oxford University Press.

References 87

[48] Salkovskis, P. M. (1985). Obsessional-compulsive problems: a cognitive-behavioural analysis. *Behaviour Research and Therapy, 23,* 571–583.

[49] Salkovskis, P. M. (1999). Understanding and treating obsessive-compulsive disorder [Special issue]. *Behaviour Research and Therapy,* S29–S52.

[50] Ishikawa, R., Kobori, O., Ikota, D., and Shimizu, E. (2014). Development and validation of the Japanese version of Responsibility Attitude Scale and Responsibility Interpretations Questionnaire. *International Journal of Culture and Mental Health,* DOI:10.1080/17542863.2014.937347.

[51] Salkovskis, P. M., Forrester, E., & Richards, C. (1998). The cognitive behavioural approach to understanding obsessional thinking. *British Journal of Psychiatry,* 173, 53-63.

[52] Salkovskis, P. M., Forrester, E., Richards, H. C., & Morrison, N. (1998). The devil is in the detail: conceptualising and treating obsessional problems. In N. Tarrier, *Cognitive therapy with complex cases.* Chichester: Wiley.

[53] Salkovskis, P. M., Wroe, A. L., Gledhill, A., Morrison, N., Forrester, E., Richards, C., et al. (2000). Responsibility attitudes and interpretations are characteristic of obsessive-compulsive disorder. *Behaviour Research and Therapy, 38,* 347–372.

[54] Coughtrey, A. E., Shafran, R., and Rachman, S. J. (2012). Imagery in mental contamination: A questionnaire study, *Journal of Obsessive-Compulsive and Related Disorders,* 2, 385–390.

[55] Fairbrother, N. and Rachman, S. (2004). Feelings of mental pollution subsequent to sexual assault. *Behaviour Research and Therapy, 40,* 173–189.

[56] Rachman, S. (1994). Pollution of the mind. *Behaviour Research and Therapy, 32,* 311–314.

[57] Bunyan, J. (1947). *An anthology. Edited by A. Stanley.* London: Eyre & Spottiswoode.

[58] Rachman, S., Radomsky, A. S., Elliott, C. M. and Zysk, E. (2012). Mental contamination: the perpetrator effect. *Journal of Behavior Therapy and Experimental Psychiatry. 43,* 587–593.

[59] Zhong, C. and Liljenquist, K. (2006). Washing away your sins: Threatened morality and physical cleansing. *Science,* 313, 1451–1452.

[60] Coughtrey, A. E., Shafran, R., Knibbs, D. and Rachman, S. J. (2012) Mental contamination in obsessive-compulsive disorder. *Journal of Obsessive-Compulsive and Related Disorders*, *1*, 244–250.

[61] Volz, C. and Heyman, I. (2007). Case series: transformation obsession in young people with obsessive-compulsive disorder (OCD). *Journal of the American Academy of Child & Adolescent Psychiatry*, 46, 766-772.

[62] Ishikawa, R., Kobori, O. & Shimizu, E. (2013). Unwanted Sexual Experiences and Cognitive Appraisals That Evoke Mental Contamination. *Behavioural and Cognitive Psychotherapy*, 1-15. doi:10.1017/S1352465813000684

[63] Fairbrother, N., Newth, S. J. and Rachman, S. (2005). Mental pollution: feelings of dirtiness without physical contact. *Behaviour Research and Therapy*, *43*, 121–130.

[64] Olatunji, B. O., Elwood, L. S., Williams, N. L. and Lohr, J. M. (2008). Mental pollution and PTSD symptoms in victims of sexual assault: a preliminary examination of the mediating role of trauma-related cognitions. *Journal of Cognitive Psychotherapy, 22,* 37–47.

[65] Berman, N. C., Wheaton, M. G., Fabricant, L. E. and Abramowitz, J. S. (2012). Predictors of mental pollution: the contribution of religion, parenting strategies, and childhood trauma. *Journal of Obsessive-Compulsive and Related Disorders, 1,* 153–158.

[66] Acierno, R., Kilpatrick, D. G. and Resnick, H. S. (1999). Posttraumatic stress disorder in adults relative to criminal victimization: prevalence, risk factors, and comorbidity. In P. A. Saigh and J. D. Bremner (Eds.), *Posttraumatic Stress Disorder: a comprehensive text* (pp. 44–68). Needham Heights, MA: Allyn and Bacon.

[67] Bachman, R. and Saltzman, L. (1995). *Violence Against Women: estimates from the redesigned survey* (NCJ Publication No. 154348). Bureau of Justice Statistics, US: Department of Justice.

[68] Hathaway, L. M., Boals, A., & Banks, J. B. (2010). PTSD symptoms and dominant emotional response to a traumatic event: An examination of DSM-IV Criterion A2. *Anxiety, Stress & Coping, 23,* 119-126.

[69] Weiss, D. S. and Marmar, C. R. (1997). The impact of event scale-revised. In J. P. Wilson and T. M. Keane (Eds.), *Assessing Psychological Trauma and PTSD*. New York: Guilford Press.

[70] Asukai, N., Kato, H., Kawamura, N., Kim, Y., Yamamoto, K., Kishimoto, et al. (2002). Reliability and validity of the Japanese-language version of the Impact of Event Scale-Revised (IES-R-J): four

studies on different traumatic events. *The Journal of Nervous and Mental Disease, 190,* 175–182.

[71] Conway, M., Mendelson, M., Giannopoulos, C., Csank, P. A. and Holm, S. L. (2004). Childhood and adult sexual abuse, rumination on sadness, and dysphoria. *Child Abuse and Neglect, 28,* 393–410.

[72] Ehlers, A., Mayou, R. A. and Bryant, B. (1998). Psychological predictors of chronic posttraumatic stress disorder after motor vehicle accidents. *Journal of Abnormal Psychology, 107,* 508–519.

[73] El Leithy, S., Brown, G. P. and Robbins, I. (2006). Counterfactual thinking and posttraumatic stress reactions. *Journal of Abnormal Psychology, 115,* 629–635.

[74] Calhoun, K. S. (1991). Treatment of rape victims: Facilitating psychosocial adjustment. New York, NY: Pergamon.

[75] Herman, J. L. (1992). Complex PTSD: A syndrome in survivors of prolonged and repeated trauma. Journal of Traumatic Stress, 5, 377-391.

[76] Steil, R, Jung, K. and Stangier, U. (2011). Efficacy of a two-session program of cognitive restructuring and imagery modification to reduce the feeling of being contaminated in adult survivors of childhood sexual abuse: a pilot study. *Journal of Behaviour Therapy and Experimental Psychiatry, 42,* 325–329.

[77] Mowrer, O. H. (1947). *On the dual nature of learning - A reinterpretation of conditioning and problem solving.* Harvard Educational Review, 17, 102e148.

[78] Coughtrey, A. E., Shafran, R., Lee, M., and Rachman, S. J. (2013). The Treatment of Mental Contamination: A Case Series. *Cognitive and Behavioral Practice* 20, 221–231

[79] Rachman S. (2010). Betrayal: a psychological analysis. *Behaviour Research and Therapy, 48,* 304-311.

[80] Radomsky, A.S., Rachman, S., Shafran, R., Coughtrey, A.E., & Barber, K.C. (2014). The nature and assessment of mental contamination: A psychometric analysis. *Journal of Obsessive Compulsive and Related Disorders, 3(2),* 181-187.

[81] Cougle, J. R., Lee, H–J., Horowitz, J.D., Wolitzky–Taylor, K. B. and Telch, M. J. (2008). An exploration of the relationship between mental pollution and OCD symptoms. *Journal of Behavior Therapy and Experimental Psychiatry, 39,* 340–353.

[82] Shafran, R., Thordarson, D. S. and Rachman, S. (1996). Thought-action fusion in obsessive-compulsive disorder. *Journal of Anxiety Disorders, 10,* 379–391.

[83] Ishikawa, R., Kobori, O. and Shimizu, E. (2014) a. *Developing the Japanese Version of the Mental Pollution Questionnaire.* Poster presented at 42nd Annual European Association for Behavioural and Cognitive Therapies, Geneva, Switzerland.

[84] Kaiser, H. and Rice, J. (1974). Little Jiffy, Mark IV, Journal of Educational and Psychological Measurement 34, 111–117.

[85] Beck, A. T., Steer, R. A., & Brown, G. K. (1996). *Manual for the Beck Depression Inventory.* Harcourt Brace: Psychological Corporation.

[86] Kojima, M., Furukawa, T. A., Takahashi, H., Kawai, M., Nagaya, T., & Tokudome, S. (2002). Cross–cultural validation of the Beck Depression Inventory–II in Japan. *Psychiatry Research,* 110, 291–299.

[87] Beck, A. T., Epstein, N., Brown, G., Steer R. A. (1988). An inventory for measuring clinical anxiety: psychometric properties. *Journal of Consulting and Clinical Psychology, 56,* 893–897.

[88] Omiya, S., Kobori, O., Tomoto, A., Igarashi, Y. and Iyo, M. (2011). Development of the Japanese version of substance use risk profile scale. *Japanese Journal of Alcohol Studies and Drug Dependence, 46,* 175.

[89] Reiss, S., Peterson, R. A., Gursky, D. M. and McNally, R. J. (1986). Anxiety sensitivity, anxiety frequency, and the prediction of fearfulness. *Behaviour Research and Therapy, 24,* 1–8.

[90] Joiner, T. E. (2001). Negative attributional style, hopelessness, depression, and endogenous depression. *Behaviour Research and Therapy,* 39, 163–173.

[91] Spoont, M. (1992). Modulatory role of serotonin in neural information processing: Implications for human psychopathology. *Psychological Bulletin,* 112, 330–350.

[92] Zuckerman, M. (1994). *Behavioural expressions and biological bases of sensation seeking.* New York: Cambridge University Press.

[93] Crocker, J., Luhtanen, R. K., Cooper, M. L., & Bouvrette, A. (2003). Contingencies of self–worth in college students: Theory and measurement. *Journal of Personality and Social Psychology,* 85, 894–908.

[94] Radomsky, A. S. and Elliott, C. M. (2009). Analyses of mental contamination: Part 2, individual differences. *Behaviour Research and Therapy, 47,* 1004–1011.

[95] Neisser, U. (1976). *Cognition and reality.* San Francisco: Freeman.

[96] Rachman, S., de Silva, P., & Roper, G. (1976). The spontaneous decay of compulsive urges. *Behaviour Research and Therapy,* 14, 445–453.

References   91

[97] de Silva, P., Menzies, R. G., Shafran, R. (2003). Spontaneous decay of compulsive urges: the case of covert compulsions. *Behaviour Research and Therapy*, 41, 129–37.

[98] Ishikawa, R., Kobori, O., Komuro, H. & Shimizu, E. (2014). Comparing the roles of washing and non-washing behaviour in the reduction of mental contamination. *Journal of Obsessive-Compulsive and Related Disorders* 3(1), 60-64.

[99] Parkinson, L., & Rachman, S. (1980). Are intrusive thoughts subject to habituation? *Behaviour Research and Therapy* 18(5) 409–418.

[100] Foa, E. B., Ehlers, A., Clark, D.M., Tolin, D. F., and Orsillo, S. M. (1999). The Posttraumatic Cognitions Inventory (PTCI). *Development and validation. Psychological Assessment,* 11, 303–314.

[101] Fennell, M. J. V. (1997). Low self–esteem: A cognitive perspective. *Behavioural and Cognitive Psychotherapy,* 25, 1–26.

[102] Boscarino J. A., & Adams, R. E. (2008). Overview of findings from the World Trade Center Disaster Outcome Study: Recommendations for future research after exposure to psychological trauma. International *Journal of Emergency Mental Health*, 10, 275–290.

[103] Briere, J., & Runtz, M. (1990). Differential adult symptomatology associated with three types of child abuse histories. Child Abuse & Neglect: *The International Journal,* 14, 357–364.

[104] Giles, M. K. (1997). Long–term consequences of sexual victimization and mediators of these consequences. Dissertation Abstracts International: Section B: *The Sciences and Engineering,* 57, 6571.

[105] Haidt, J., McCauley, C., Rozin, P. (2002). *Disgust scale, Version 2, Short form.* from http://people.virginia.edu/~jdh6n/disgustscale. html.

[106] Crocker, J., Luhtanen, R. K., Cooper, M. L., & Bouvrette, A. (2003). Contingencies of self-worth in college students: Theory and measurement. *Journal of Personality and Social Psychology*, 85, 894-908.

[107] Rosenberg, M. (1965). *Society and the adolescent self–image.* Princeton, NJ: Princeton University Press.

[108] Mimura, C, & Griffiths, P. A. (2007). Japanese version of the Rosenberg self–esteem scale: translation and equivalence assessment. *Journal of Psychosomatic Research,* 62, 589–94.

[109] Uchida, T., & Ueno, T. (2010). Reliability and validity of the Rosenberg Self Esteem Scale: using the Japanese version of the RSES by Mimura & Griffiths (2007). *The Annual Reports of the Faculty of Education, Tohoku University,* 58, 257–266.

[110] Zeigler–Hill, V., & Abraham, J. (2006). Borderline personality features: Instability of self–esteem and affect. *Journal of Social and Clinical Psychology,* 25, 668–687.

[111] Baer, L., Jenike, M. A., Black, D. W., Treece, C., Rosenfeld, R., & Greist, J. (1992). Effect of axis II disorders on treatment outcome with clomipramine in 55 patients with obsessive–compulsive disorder. *Archives of General Psychiatry* 49, 862–866.

[112] Kuppens, P., Van Mechelen, I., Smits, D. J. M., De Boeck, P., & Ceulemas, E. (2007). Individual differences in patterns of appraisal and anger experience. *Cognition & Emotion,* 21, 68−713.

[113] Fennell, M. J. V. (1999). *Overcoming low self–esteem: A self–help guide using cognitive behavioural techniques.* London: Robinson Publishing.

[114] Bennett–Levy, J., Butler, G., Fennell, M. J. V., Hackmann, A., Mueller, M., & Westbrook, D. (Eds.) (2004). The Oxford guide to behavioural experiments in cognitive therapy. Oxford: Oxford University Press.

[115] Foa, E. B., Keane, T. M. & Friedman, M. J. (2000). Effective Treatments for PTSD : *Practice Guidelines from the International Society for Traumatic Stress Studies.* Guilford Press: New York.

[116] Cohen, J.A., Mannarino, A.P., & Deblinger, E. (2006). *Treating trauma and traumatic grief in children and adolescents.* New York: Guilford Press.

[117] Cohen, J. A., Deblinger, E., Mannarino, A. P., & Steer, R. (2004). A multisite, randomized controlled trial for children with sexual abuse-related PTSD symptoms. *Journal of the American Academy of Child & Adolescent Psychiatry*, 43, 393-402.

[118] Cohen, J. A., & Mannarino, A. P. (1996). A treatment outcome study for sexually abused preschool children: Initial findings. *Journal of the American Academy of Child and Adolescent Psychiatry,* 35(1), 42-50.

[119] Cohen, J. A., & Mannarino, A. P. (1997). A treatment study of sexually abused preschool children: Outcome during one year follow-up. *Journal of the American Academy of Child and Adolescent Psychiatry* 36(9), 1228-1235.

[120] Cohen, J. A., Mannarino, A. P., & Knudsen K. (2005). Treating sexually abused children: One year follow-up of a randomized controlled trial. *Child Abuse & Neglect,* 29, 135-146.

[121] Deblinger, E., Mannarino, A. P., Cohen, J. A., Runyon, M. K., & Steer, R. A. (2011). Trauma-Focused Cognitive Behavioral Therapy for

children: Impact of the trauma narrative and treatment length. *Depression and Anxiety,* 28, 67–75.

[122] Deblinger, E., Mannarino, A. P., Cohen, J. A., & Steer, R. A. (2006). A multisite, randomized controlled trial for children with sexual abuse-related PTSD symptoms: Examining predictors of treatment response. *Journal of the American Academy of Child and Adolescent Psychiatry,* 45, 1474-1484.

[123] Deblinger, E., Stauffer, L., & Steer, R. (2001). Comparative efficacies of supportive and cognitive behavioral group therapies for children who were sexually abused and their nonoffending mothers. Child Maltreatment 6(4), 332-343.

[124] Deblinger, E., Steer, R. A., & Lippmann, J. (1999). Two year follow-up study of cognitive behavioral therapy for sexually abused children suffering post-traumatic stress symptoms. *Child Abuse and Neglect,* 23(12), 1371-1378.

[125] Warnock-Parkes, E., Salkovskis, P. M., & Rachman, S. J. (2012). When the problem is beneath the surface in OCD: The cognitive treatment of a case of pure mental contamination. *Behavioural and Cognitive Psychotherapy,* 40, 383–399.

[126] Rachman, S. J., Shafran, R., Mitchell, D., Trant, J., & Teachman, B. (1996). How to remain neutral: An experimental analysis of neutralisation. *Behaviour Research and Therapy,* 34, 889–898.

[127] Salkovskis, P. M., Bass, C. (1997). *Hypochondriasis. In The Science and Practice of Cognitive Behaviour Therapy (eds Clark & Fairburn).* Oxford: Oxford University Press.

[128] Salkovskis, P. M., & Kirk, J. (1997). *Obsessive-compulsive disorder.* In D. M. Clark & C. Fairburn (Eds.), The science and practice of cognitive behaviour therapy. Oxford: Oxford University Press.

[129] Wild, J., & Clark, D. M. (2011). Imagery rescripting of early traumatic memories in social phobia. Cognitive and Behavioural Practice, 18, 433–443

[130] Holmes, E. A., Arntz, A., & Smucker, M. R. (2007). Imagery rescripting in cognitive and behaviour therapy: Images, treatment techniques and outcomes. *Journal of Behavior Therapy and Experimental Psychiatry,* 38, 297-305.

[131] Wolff, K., Goldsmith, S. I., Katz, L. A., Gilchrest, B. A., Paller, A. S., & Leffell, D. J. (2007*). Fitzpatrick's dermatology in general medicine.* Columbus, OH: McGraw-Hill

[132] Foa, E. B., Dancu, C. V., Hembree, E. A., Jaycox, L. H., Meadows, E. A., & Street, G. P. (1999). A comparison of exposure therapy, stress inoculation training, and their combination for reducing posttraumatic stress disorder in female assault victims. *Journal of Consulting and Clinical Psychology*, 67, 194–200.

[133] Resick, P. A., Nishith, P., Weaver, T. L., Astin, M. C., & Feuer, C. A. (2002). A comparison of cognitive-processing therapy with prolonged exposure and a waiting condition for the treatment of chronic posttraumatic stress disorder in female rape victims. *Journal of Consulting and Clinical Psychology,* 70, 867–879.

[134] Schnurr, P. P., Friedman, M. J., Engel, C. C., Foa, E. B., Shea, M. T., Chow, B. K., et al. (2007). Cognitive behavioral therapy for posttraumatic stress disorder in women: a randomized controlled trial. *The Journal of the American Medical Association, 297*, 820–830.

[135] Bryant, R. A., Moulds, M. L., Guthrie, R. M., Dang, S. T., Mastrodomenico, J., Nixon, R. D. V., et al. (2008). A randomized controlled trial of exposure therapy and cognitive restructuring for posttraumatic stress disorder. *Journal of Consulting and Clinical Psychology,* 76, 695–703.

[136] Powers, M. B., Halpern, J. M., Ferenschak, M. P., Gillihan, S. J., & Foa, E. B. (2010). A meta-analytic review of prolonged exposure for posttraumatic stress disorder. *Clinical Psychology Review,* 30, 635–641.

[137] American Psychiatric Association. (2013) *Diagnostic and statistical manual of mental disorders,* (5th ed.). Washington, DC: Author.

[138] Foa, E. B. and Kozak, M. J. (1986). Emotional processing of fear: exposure to corrective information. *Psychological Bulletin*, 99, 20-35.

INDEX

A

acute phase, 3

B

behavioral experiments, 25, 71, 74, 76, 79
betrayal, 21, 23, 25, 37

C

cognitive behavioral therapy (CBT), 25, 72
cognitive restructuring and imagery, 71, 78, 79, 89
cognitive theory of OCD, 11
cognitive theory of PTSD, 7

D

depression, 42
disgust towards perpetrator's body fluids, 48
disorganized trauma memories, 1, 7

E

ecological validity, 53

F

fear of morphing, 25, 26
forcible touching/frottage, 29, 30, 31, 32

I

inflated sense of responsibility, 18, 20, 39, 41, 42, 45, 47, 49
internal negative emotions, 29, 33, 47, 57

L

low self-esteem, 63, 68, 69

M

mental contamination, vii, 21, 22, 23, 24, 25, 27, 29, 30, 31, 32, 34, 35, 37, 38, 45, 47, 48, 49, 50, 51, 53, 54, 55, 56, 57, 58, 59, 61, 62, 63, 64, 68, 69, 71, 74, 75, 76, 77, 78, 79, 81, 86, 87, 89, 90, 91, 93

mental pollution questionnaire, 38
morality, 50

N

neat freaks, 11, 13
negative appraisals after traumatization, 48
negative appraisals of trauma memories, 1, 7
neutralizing behaviors, 18, 56

O

obsessive-compulsive disorder (OCD), 88
obsessive-compulsive inventory, 85
Obsessive-Compulsive Inventory, 15
ordinary sense of dirtiness, 23, 24, 37, 55, 74

P

Padua Inventory, 15, 16, 86

R

reassurance-seeking behaviors, 13

responsibility attitudes, 19, 20
responsibility interpretation, 19

S

sexual assault, vii, 1, 2, 3, 4, 5, 9, 21, 23, 25, 27, 28, 29, 30, 31, 32, 34, 35, 45, 61, 64, 71, 79, 83, 84, 87, 88
spontaneously decay, 57, 62
substance use risk profile scale, 90

T

thought-action fusion, 37, 49

U

unwanted sexual experiences, vii, 27, 28, 29, 30, 32, 33, 34, 35, 47, 49, 50, 53

V

verbal sexual assault, 29, 30, 31, 32, 35
violation, 5, 47, 49, 50, 51, 52, 53, 54, 64, 68
virtue subscale, 43
visual sexual assault, 27, 29, 30, 31, 32, 34, 35